Olivier Messiaen
and the
Tristan Myth

Olivier Messiaen
and the
Tristan Myth

Audrey Ekdahl Davidson

PRAEGER

Westport, Connecticut
London

Library of Congress Cataloging-in-Publication Data

Davidson, Audrey Ekdahl.
　Olivier Messiaen and the Tristan myth / by Audrey Ekdahl Davidson.
　　p. cm.
　Includes bibliographical references and index.
　ISBN 0–275–97340–9 (alk. paper)
　　1. Messiaen, Olivier, 1908—Criticism and interpretation. 2. Tristan (Legendary character)—Songs and music—History and criticism. 3. Iseult (Legendary character)—Songs and music—History and criticism. I. Title.
ML410.M595D38 2001
780'.92—dc21   2001032912

British Library Cataloguing in Publication Data is available.

Copyright © 2001 by Audrey Ekdahl Davidson

All rights reserved. No portion of this book may be reproduced, by any process or technique, without the express written consent of the publisher.

Library of Congress Catalog Card Number: 2001032912
ISBN: 0–275–97340–9

First published in 2001

Praeger Publishers, 88 Post Road West, Westport, CT 06881
An imprint of Greenwood Publishing Group, Inc.
www.praeger.com

Printed in the United States of America

The paper used in this book complies with the Permanent Paper Standard issued by the National Information Standards Organization (Z39.48–1984).

10 9 8 7 6 5 4 3 2 1

Copyright Acknowledgments

The author and publisher gratefully acknowledge permission for use of the following material:

Material from Audrey Ekdahl Davidson, "Olivier Messiaen's *Cinq Rechants*: The Conclusion of His Tristan Trilogy," *The Centennial Review* 25 (Winter 1981), 48–58. Used by permission of Michigan State University Press.

Material from Audrey Ekdahl Davidson, "Messiaen's Use of Peruvian Sources in His *Harawi* Song Cycle," *Michigan Academician* 12 (Summer 1979), 47–59. Used by permission.

Material from C.G. Jung, *The Psychology of Transference*, vol. 16. Copyright © 1966 by the Bollingen Foundation. Reprinted by permission of Princeton University Press.

Excerpts from André Breton, "L'Union Libre," in *Poems*, edited and translated by Jean-Pierre Cauvin and Mary Ann Caws (Austin: University of Texas Press, 1982), 48–51. Used by permission of the translators and the original publisher, Gallimard.

Quoted material and musical examples from Olivier Messiaen's *Cinq rechants* (Paris: Rouart, Lerolle [distr. Éditions Salabert], 1949). © 1960 Rouart-Lerolle/Salabert. With kind authorization of Éditions Salabert.

Quoted material and musical examples from Olivier Messiaen's *Harawi* (Paris: Alphonse Leduc, 1948). Used by permission of Alphonse Leduc and Mme. Messiaen.

Hieronymus Bosch, central panel, *The Garden of Earthly Delights*. Museo del Prado, Madrid. Alinari/Art Resource, NY.

Musical examples from Olivier Messiaen's *Turangalîla-symphonie*. © 1992 Éditions Durand. Used by permission.

Quoted material and musical examples from *La Musique des Incas et ses survivances*, edited by Marguerite and Raoul d'Harcourt (Paris: Paul Geuthner). Used by permission.

Every reasonable effort has been made to trace the owners of copyright materials in this book, but in some instances this has proven impossible. The author and publisher will be glad to receive information leading to more complete acknowledgments in subsequent printings of the book and in the meantime extend their apologies for any omissions.

Contents

Preface	ix
1 The Composer and the Myth	1
2 *Harawi: Song of Love and Death*	23
3 *Turangalîla-symphonie*: The Cosmic Dimension of Love	63
4 *Cinq rechants*: The Lovers Fly Away	107
Bibliography	133
Index	139

Preface

Olivier Messiaen's reputation as a giant among twentieth-century composers would not be what it is without his organ works, his *Quartet for the End of Time*, and the three works—*Harawi, Turangalîla-symphonie*, and *Cinq rechants*—which make up his Tristan trilogy. The organ works expressed his deep religious faith, while in the quartet this faith was joined with the terror of his personal experience in the concentration camp at Görlitz in 1940–41. The Tristan trilogy germinated after his release from imprisonment and his return to teaching, and, like the quartet, it represents his most mature work.

I first became aware of Messiaen's music thirty-five years ago when I was asked to translate into English an article on *La Nativité du Seigneur* by the German church composer Heinz Werner Zimmermann. Zimmermann observed in that article that "in Messiaen's method of constructing melodies, we find a technique of astonishing originality." Hearing Messiaen's organ works played by my friend and colleague the late Kathryn Loew confirmed the ingeniousness of his modal practice and his use of non-Western rhythms. Together we performed on one occasion the *Harawi* song cycle. And as a topic for my dissertation that would fit my need for a medieval-modern topic, Messiaen's Tristan trilogy seemed to be a natural choice. For my advisor, I was fortunate to have the late

Johannes Riedel, who encouraged me and gave me the freedom I needed. The present book, written a quarter of a century later, could not have been produced without drawing on the work that I did for my dissertation.

My principal debt is to my husband, Clifford Davidson, who was virtually a collaborator in the present project. During a continuing period of my ill health, he not only has given support but has actively helped in essential ways. Although not a musician, he has brought his long experience as an editor to bear in invaluable ways. I have also received encouragement and assistance in various ways from many others. I cannot name them all, but I must mention Jeremy Ribando, who set up the musical examples on his computer, and David Collins, whose assistance with French texts was indispensable.

Figure 1. Roland Penrose, *The Invisible Isle* (1936).

Figure 2. Hieronymus Bosch (c. 1450–1516), central panel, *The Garden of Earthly Delights*. Museo del Prado, Madrid. Alinari/Art Resource, NY.

1

The Composer and the Myth

The story of Tristan (Tristram) and Iseult (Isolde) concerns one of the most famous love triangles of all time. Derived from Celtic sources, it has retained its setting in Celtic lands—Brittany, Cornwall, and Ireland. Its earliest version is now lost, but the fundamental episodes were transmitted by Thomas of Brittany (1150–70), Béroul and Eilhart (1170–90), and Gottfried von Strassburg (ca. 1210).[1] The latter's uncompleted German poem is the principal source of Richard Wagner's music-drama *Tristan und Isolde*, which subsequently was a principal inspiration for Olivier Messiaen (1908–92) for three of his most remarkable compositions.

Though Messiaen is reported by his second wife, Yvonne Loriod, to have said, "I am a composer of the Middle Ages,"[2] the Tristan story is not one that we would expect to have appealed to him. Messiaen was known prior to 1945, the final year of World War II, primarily as a Catholic organist, the incumbent at the Church of the Holy Trinity in Paris, and as a composer of religious music. However, in June through September of that year he completed his first composition based on the Tristan story, *Harawi*,[3] a song cycle and the first in a trilogy that ultimately would also include *Turangalîla-symphonie* and *Cinq rechants*, both completed in 1948. These represented a distinct departure in subject matter

2 Olivier Messiaen and the Tristan Myth

from his previous compositions but would involve music that, up to this point, he regarded as some of his best work.[4] Needless to say, Messiaen's Tristan trilogy not only revealed a surprising side of his character, but also meant the application of his own previously developed musical language to secular compositions of very great stature.

Messiaen's work before 1945 reveals a composer whose life seems to have found its center in the expression of his Christian faith, which remained with him to the end of his life and which for him was associated with joy.[5] The great work of his final years was his opera *Saint François d'Assise*, upon which he labored for eight years.[6] Messiaen had said in an interview with Claude Samuel, "The first idea that I wanted to express . . . is the existence of the truths of the Catholic faith." He added, "I was born a believer."[7] In an address given upon his receipt of the Erasmus Prize in Amsterdam in 1971, he proclaimed his belief in God: "And because I believe in God, I believe likewise in the Holy Trinity and in the Holy Spirit . . . and in the Son, the Word made Flesh, Jesus Christ (to whom I've dedicated a large part of my works)."[8] His early organ works, which have been widely admired for the mystical qualities of their music, were given titles such as *Le Banquet céleste* (1928), *L'Ascension* (1933), *La Nativité du Seigneur* (1935), and *Les Corps glorieux* (1939). As a general rule, he either prefaced these works with his own explanations setting forth the programmatic nature of the music or provided appropriate biblical texts, which are intended to illuminate their intended theological and mystical associations. He aimed for dazzling coloristic effects in his religious music—the kind of music that "shakes our sensibilities into motion, pushes us to go beyond concepts, to approach that which is higher than reason and intuition, that is to say FAITH."[9]

But even in compositions not written for the organ—e.g., *Quatuor pour la fin du temps* (*Quartet for the End of Time*), composed in 1940–41 while he was in the German prison camp at Görlitz in Silesia—the religious implications are not abandoned. If anything, the programmatic basis of the quartet, which presents to us the apocalyptic angel who announces the end of Time (derived from Revelation 10:5–7), is even more urgently theological and eschatologically oriented. It is a sign of Messiaen's piety that the angel is more beloved than a figure of terror.[10] The angel descends in the second movement of the quartet against the background of the "impalpable harmonies of heaven"; he is "clothed with a cloud: and a rainbow was upon his head, and his face was as it were the sun, and his feet on the sea and the earth" (Rev. 10:1). In the seventh move-

The Composer and the Myth

ment, the angel is spectacularly enveloped by a rainbow, which is symbolic of peace, wisdom, and "all luminous and sonorous vibrations."[11]

The sacred intrudes even in the three secular vocal cycles written by Messiaen before World War II. *Trois Mélodies* (1930), which includes a setting of a poem, "Le sourire," by his mother as the central song—framed by his own verses at the beginning and end of the cycle—concludes in his final song, "La fiancée perdue," with a cry to Jesus to bless the lost one and to give her repose. *Poèmes pour Mi* (1936–37) was written for his first wife, Claire Delbos, whom he had given the nickname "Mi."[12] Here Messiaen speaks of love between man and woman, of the sacrament of marriage, of the birth of a child, and of the relationship between God and man. Thus in his religious faith he, like the medieval artisans who were totally enveloped by their religious experience, had made what would seem to be a wholeness of his life and art. No artificial line could be drawn between sacred and profane. All aspects of human life—indeed, all human relationships—are ultimately held in God's hand, as in Auguste Rodin's *Hand of God* sculpture (1898).[13] However, closer scrutiny of the poems and music does not always seem to bear out this integrated vision. One notices the surrealistic and even nightmarish quality of the poems, especially "Épouvante," which begins and ends with a demonic laugh. Tremendous anxiety is evidenced here as in the words "Des lambeaux sanglants te suivraient dans les ténébres" ("The bloody shreds would follow you into the dark").[14] Antoine Goléa has commented that this song "has the look of a medieval treatise on sorcery where one confuses the wounds, physically inflicted on the body by the loved one, with the marks of the devil."[15]

It would appear that for Messiaen at this time, marriage and its relationship between a man and a woman involved not only peaceful moments but also an anguished fear of loss of love. Then at the end of the cycle he seems to escape altogether from such negative feelings: the husband stands alone in prayer before God, to whom he appeals for the healing of his own soul. Likewise, the final song in *Chants de Terre et de Ciel* (1938) draws back from the physical relationships of the earlier part of the cycle. The movement is toward the transcendent, even the mystical. Messiaen's poetry here speaks of Christ's Resurrection, the angel seated at the empty tomb, and the divinely resurrected Son of God who sings praises to the Father as he surrealistically ascends to him. Musically, at this point in the cycle, a very sophisticated kind of word painting appears that indicates upward movement.

Messiaen's musical technique in these two song cycles is already well formed and mature in his use of modes, nonretrogradable and added rhythms, favorite melodic intervals including the tritone, chords of superpositions, and chords with added notes. In *The Technique of My Musical Language* (1944) he wrote: "The two cycles for voice and piano entitled *Poèmes pour Mi* and *Chants de Terre et de Ciel* have unfortunately been quoted very little in the present work. Since they are particularly 'true' in sentiment and typical of my manner, I advise the reader who desires to understand my music better to begin by reading them."[16] While the composer's art foreshadows what was to come, there is no unfolding of emotion and no development of a large mythic structure such as he was to produce in his Tristan trilogy.

Retrospective examination of these earlier works, then, presents signs of the ensuing abrupt change in Messiaen's consciousness that would be revealed in his Tristan trilogy. Already there was the tortured expression of physical love, which seemed then merely to interrupt or impair the relationship between man and the divine. In his previous desire to escape from the physical to a metaphysical existence, he had proclaimed that life in its most carnal sense was a problem to be solved or transcended. The language of psychology speaks of repression that gives way to a surge of emotion that breaks through into a new experience after which nothing can be quite the same. A metamorphosis from such strict and ascetic religiosity that makes love difficult on a purely human level, to a glorification of human passions such as we have in the Tristan story, is perhaps in these terms not to be seen as particularly unusual. But why did he find his aesthetic solution, the objective correlative for his emotion, in the myth of Tristan and Iseult? For here is a medieval story that hardly can be considered to be within the religious framework of Christianity. Here sin and guilt would seem to dominate—not resurrected and glorified bodies. It seems a strange subject for one who continued to say of himself, "I am above all a Catholic musician. All my works, *religious or not*, are an act of faith and glorify the mystery of Christ."[17] "I have wanted," he said elsewhere, "to express the marvels of Faith."[18] But from the standpoint of a strictly Catholic moral theology, it would seem that Tristan and Iseult must be labeled immoral; their behavior as described in the medieval accounts would appear antithetical to the deep faith, liturgical piety, and strict morality espoused by Messiaen. Dante, the great Catholic poet, explicitly placed Tristan with the lustful in the second circle of hell (*Inferno*, 5:67), where he nevertheless swoons with pity for the lovers at the end of the canto. Yet the story of Tristan and Iseult as it appears traditionally is not entirely unrelated to the religious point of view, for a deep sense of guilt or sin can exist only if one has lived within the structure of a strong personal ethic, whether or not that ethic is Christian.

The change in Messiaen's life that made possible his Tristan trilogy coincided with a personal crisis. Tanneguy de Quénetain has written that, while Messiaen hated any probing of his privacy during his lifetime, his personal life is relevant to a discussion of his composition:

> But can one really bypass completely the drama of his personal life and problems if one wants to grasp the true nature of the man and his work? The fact is that, during the war, his wife fell ill with a serious disease of the brain which first attacked her mental faculties. Transferred to a nursing home she slowly wasted away, and by 1959 all her faculties, including those of hearing, sight and the ability to move her limbs, had gone.
>
> Absolutely cut off from his wife by this illness, but indissolubly tied to her by the marriage sacrament (Messiaen's religious convictions were. . . . very strict), he met in his class at the Conservatoire "an inspired, sublime and unique pianist": Yvonne Loriod. It was then that he composed his great works for the piano. . . . In addition, . . . he composed the *Harawi, chant d'amour et de mort*, the *Turangalîla-symphonie* and the *Cinq rechants*, three works glorifying profane love that drew inspiration from the Tristan myth—the supreme myth of passionate love which a transcendent veto causes to remain unconsummated, and which finds fulfillment only in death.[19]

While the medieval accounts of such writers as Thomas of Brittany, Béroul and Eilhart, and Gottfried von Strassburg emphasized the sensuality of the lovers, Messiaen, in an interview with Claude Samuel, insisted upon the unconsummated nature of the love between his Tristan and Iseult. He insisted that in his work he had treated "a greater and purer love"—a love in which the lovers are entrapped and which may not lead to satisfaction of their desire. "I'm thinking," said Messiaen, "of the enchanted tower in which Vivian imprisons Merlin."[20] Such remarks, however, seem to apply better to *Harawi* or *Cinq rechants* than to the *Turangalîla-symphonie*. The fifth movement of the symphony celebrates an ecstatic and even orgiastic expression of love.

Messiaen's personal experiences, whatever they were, thus meant a

6   Olivier Messiaen and the Tristan Myth

discovery of his own humanity. His own words are revealing: "The illumination of the theological truths of the Catholic faith is the first aspect
of my work. . . . *But I am a human being,* and like all others I am susceptible to human love, which I wished to express in three of my works that
incorporate the greatest myth of human love, that of Tristan and
Iseult."[21] The myth adopted by him involved the distancing of material
that is thus made impersonal, and it made possible his engagement with
the problems of love leading to death—and involving sacrifice and re-
nunciation. This love, which derives from the deepest resources of the
human personality and which grasps one with a force beyond one's
will—a force symbolized in the ancient story by the love potion—is
marked by anguish as well as joy. The concept of the "abyss," with which
he had been earlier fascinated in his *Quatuor pour la fin du temps,* now in
the Tristan trilogy becomes a complex symbol; among other significa-
tions, it implies despair and anguish as the lover is caught in the triangle
of love. The anguish was both personal and expressed in his art, as he
seems to have admitted when he said, "I have had plenty of unhappiness
in my life, plenty."[22] The abyss, as visualized so dramatically, for example, in *Turangalîla-symphonie,* is an archetypal symbol for the most
primitive level of man's experience;[23] in Messiaen's work it clearly is a
highly complicated piece of symbolism. But certainly for him it is something that can hardly be miraculously escaped from or avoided; rather,
a "coming through" the abyss is demanded—a "coming through" that
eventually means a kind of healing experience after long pain.

    Messiaen's primary source for the Tristan and Iseult myth seems not
to have been the early romances, though he knew something of the au-
thentic medieval versions of the story, but rather the artist whom Mallarmé had called "Le dieu Richard Wagner irradiant un sacre."[24] The
texts that Messiaen himself created for *Harawi* and *Cinq rechants* are, however, not structured as a narrative. Instead the verses which he provided
involve a poetry that, like symbolist and Surrealist poetry as well as
Surrealist painting, arranges seemingly disjunctive images around a central mythic or archetypal idea.[25] He thus finds his place in the main-
stream of French artistic practice of the preceding hundred years:

> Already in the nineteenth century Rimbaud had attempted to sep-
> arate words from their intellectual functions and conventional
> meanings. . . . Then Mallarmé . . . further liberated words from their
> conventional senses. Enormously influential in modern European
> literature, Mallarmé distinguished between "immediate speech"—

The Composer and the Myth 7

for the rational uses of everyday existence—and "essential speech" to deal with the essence of things.... Mallarmé attempted to use words and syllables, free of "worn-out, rational meanings," to give "a purer sense to the words of the tribe" and to affect readers in a nonrational way. He attempted consciously to use language in poetry as composers use sound in music, and not for sound alone but ... as "emotional metaphors."[26]

In *Harawi* and *Cinq rechants* Messian thus not only attempted to make fresh connections between words already in the French language but also borrowed from other languages—Quechua and Sanskrit. Furthermore, especially in *Cinq rechants*, he even made up his own language; for example, he invented words such as "hayoma kapritama,"[27] which appear to be made up of Quechua or Sanskrit syllables but which are in fact entirely synthetic. But it is in a larger sense that these compositions— and *Turangalîla-symphonie* as well—are Surrealistic masterpieces, for they were as disruptive with regard to the proprieties of the concert hall as was the poetry of the Surrealist poets to the prevailing academic understanding of the nature of poetry.[28]

Messiaen alternately denied and admitted his affinities with the Surrealist movement. He preferred the French term *surnaturel* to describe his work: "there are three categories [of styles]—the *real*, the *surreal*, and the *supernatural* [*surnaturel*], and I think I have passed these others and have attained the supernatural."[29] But elsewhere he more frankly admitted the affinities at least between his verse and the Surrealist style. "I have been a great reader and admirer of Pierre Reverdy and Paul Éluard," he said; "I am, therefore, some sort of surrealist in the poems for my works, if not in my music."[30]

From the Surrealists Messiaen apparently took his practice of linking together seemingly unrelated images (e.g., the stringing together of the images of water, time, and heaven in "L'escalier redit, gestes du soleil," Song 9 in *Harawi*). The Surrealists had developed this linking technique from the psychoanalytic theories of Sigmund Freud, whose ideas about the subconscious mind and about the use of free association to probe that previously unexplored area became very influential in the arts. The Surrealist painters and poets, under Freud's influence, wanted to tap the resources of their own unconscious minds and of their dreams and to use that material in their art. André Breton, whom Messiaen greatly admired,[31] even attempted automatic writing. Others turned to their fantasies and dreams as sources for visual images. They distrusted rational,

8 Olivier Messiaen and the Tristan Myth

logical ways of linking words and symbolic images and looked instead to their inner selves and their emotions for their poetic and painterly insights.

The way had been well prepared for the Surrealist method of working by the earlier symbolist poets, especially by Mallarmé, who believed that "*to name* an object is to destroy three-quarters of the enjoyment of a poem, which is made up of the pleasure of guessing little by little; *to suggest it*—that is the ideal."[32] His creative practice seems to have foreshadowed both Messiaen's practice of making word associations and of creating musical connections. "I have found," said Mallarmé, "an intimate and peculiar manner of depicting and setting down very fugitive impressions. What is frightening is that all these impressions are required to be woven together as in a symphony, and that I often spend whole days wondering whether one idea can be associated with another, what the relationship between them may be, and what effect they will create."[33]

Many of Messiaen's images in the Tristan trilogy are ones that appear over and over in Surrealist painting and poetry. For example, the bird, one of his most significant images, was also important as a symbol for Max Ernst—so important that the painter called himself "Loplop, Superior of the Birds."[34] Stars appear again and again in Messiaen's verses and in the Surrealists' paintings. Blue skies with cottony clouds are juxtaposed with soft watches crawling with bugs in Salvador Dali's well-known *Persistence of Memory*—a juxtaposition echoed in Messiaen's linkage of "Ciel" and "Temps." Hands and heads are also important in Messiaen's work, especially in Song 10 of *Harawi*, "Amour oiseau d'étoile," which was inspired by an illustration in a Swiss journal showing a Surrealist painting, Roland Penrose's lost *The Invisible Isle* (see Figure 1, located after Preface).

Nahma Sandrow observes that the "drive basic to surrealism is toward . . . a reconciliation of opposites" such as irrationality and higher rational order.[35] Thus in the poetry of *Harawi*, the finite and infinite, the irrational and rational are brought together. In Song 11, Messiaen, in a nonsyntactical construction, writes, "Katchikatchi les étoiles" ("grasshopper the stars"), hence transferring the dancing and leaping (*sauter*) quality of these insects to the stars. At the same time, underneath these images is a larger reconciliation: the lovers, who have previously experienced anguish as well as joy, now are transformed into joyful stars, which exist beyond anxiety and discomfort. For Messiaen as well as the Surrealists, "reconciliation [is] an intensification in time as well as in spirit, a way

The Composer and the Myth   9

to assimilate Bergsonian duration in time. The tension inherent in the willed unification of opposites which are straining apart [lends] a kind of quivering energy."[36]

Messiaen was very modest about the quality of his verse: "My poems are made with the music and for the music. They have no other literary pretensions."[37] Yet it should be noted that his family had been talented in literature. His mother, the poet Cécile Sauvage, had even written a cycle of poems entitled L'Ame en bourgeon before his birth in which she had spoken in lyrical terms of the coming into existence of a new life: "Des cheveux blonds sur front bombé, des yeux noisette, des yeux riants, parlants, chantants, pensants, un drôle de petit nez carré, une belle fossette . . . sur la joue."[38] His father was a teacher of English literature and a translator of Shakespeare, while his brother Alain was also a poet. Olivier Messiaen's own verse has, to be sure, received little praise from critics. It is a poetry, however, that is not expected to stand alone. His verse, as he himself explains, is secondary to the music—but it is nevertheless essential to its expression.

While Messiaen's verse proceeds in an apparently non-narrative fashion, it nevertheless provides the necessary verbal referents that point to given elements of the myth utilized in the Tristan trilogy. Unlike other composers who worked with a previously completed libretto or poetic text, Messiaen here and elsewhere normally composed the music and wrote the words simultaneously. In an interview with the German composer Heinz Werner Zimmermann, he explained that "in his vocal music, text and musical setting are produced at the same time, whereby the music sensitively takes into account the word accents."[39] Both text and music therefore are in a sense *wound around the myth* in a kind of analysis of the myth. The words and music together serve to mediate between the myth and a logical explanation of it.[40] A logical explanation would lay it out flat, like making a flat map out of a globe. Messiaen's way was to wrap words and music around the armature of the myth, hence proceeding in a way analogous to the sculptor creating a piece of additive sculpture. The result, then, is a composition that is intended accurately to show off the design and the contours of the essential myth at the center.

The *musical* procedure adopted by Messiaen in the Tristan trilogy actually owes much more than its story to Wagner. It has been claimed that Wagner was "the undeniable originator of the structural analysis of myths . . . *in music*," and that he made the "discovery that the structure of myths can be revealed through a musical score."[41] But Messiaen goes further in that he attempts to reveal even more directly (not only in music, but also in the words set to music) the contours of the myth. Within each of the twelve songs of *Harawi*, for example, he attacks separate mythic and hence musical problems as these are found in the mythic material. Similarly, the separate movements of *Turangalîla-symphonie* (where, since it is a symphony, there is no setting of a text) and the five parts of *Cinq rechants* each present one-third of a larger solution toward which the composer has been building throughout the trilogy.

While, as noted, the principal inspiration for the use of the Tristan myth was Wagner's music drama *Tristan und Isolde*, Messiaen also will be seen to have added a great deal to his original material through the use of other sources, including a Peruvian analogue. In *Harawi* Isolde/Iseult is even changed into Piroutcha, from Peruvian folklore, though she appears again under her own name, conventionally spelled "Yseult," in *Cinq rechants*. Messiaen was not setting out to remake *Tristan und Isolde* but to create an entirely different kind of work, which would be unique in its own way.[42] In *Harawi* he begins *in medias res*, utilizing the material that Wagner had put into Act 2 of his music drama. The lovers are already under the spell of the love potion to which Wagner had devoted his entire first act. References to the potion appear: Messiaen calls it a "philtre à deux voix" in the seventh and ninth songs of *Harawi*, and there are also allusions to it in *Cinq rechants*.[43] The mechanics of the love potion interest him less than the fatal and irresistible nature of passion. The potion is not a cause of love so much as a symbol: "Fatal love, irresistible, which transcends all, which suppresses all except itself, which is symbolized by the philter of Tristan and Isolde."[44]

The lovers in the crucial second act of Wagner's music drama meet in a garden for a love duet of unparalleled length and intensity. Messiaen retains the garden imagery, though fragmented and combined with material from the Song of Songs and Bosch's painting *The Garden of Earthly Delights*. In Act 2, scene 2, of Wagner's drama, the lovers, who have surreptitiously met in the dark of the night, sink down on a flowery bank: "*Tristan zieht Isolde sanft zur Seite auf eine Blumenbank nieder, senkt sich vor ihr auf die Knie und schmiegt sein Haupt in ihren Arm*" ("*Tristan takes Isolde and lays her down on the bank of flowers; he falls on his knees before her and places his head on her arm*").[45] Messiaen borrowed the "Blumenbank" as "le banc" in the first song of *Harawi* in "a poetic transposition very simple and very direct of the scenery of the second act of Wagner's *Tristan*."[46] In Act 1, scene 5, Wagner described the lovers as having their

The Composer and the Myth   11

glances caught on one another: *"Dann suchen sie sich wieder mit dem Blick, senken ihn verwirrt und heften ihn wieder mit steigender Sehnsucht aufeinander"* (*"They gaze at each other, fall into confusion, and then look increasingly lovingly at each other"*).[47] These glances too are translated by Messiaen into "L'oeil immobile, sans dénouer ton regard" ("Eyes immobile, without unraveling your glance") in the first song of *Harawi*.

The most moving section of the second act of Wagner's music drama involves an *alba*, as Brangäne, like the watchman in the medieval dawn song or *alba*, warns the lovers to be on their guard. Here the quietude of love is combined with the danger of discovery. In *Harawi*, as we will see, a remarkable transformation takes place, since Brangäne's role in the *alba* is taken over by the monkeys who warn the prince of danger by passing the word "pia" from one to another and from tree to tree.[48] Also, Brangäne is brought back in *Cinq rechants*, where the text announces: "Les amoureux s'envolent, Brangien dans l'espace tu souffles" ("The lovers fly away, Brangäne, once in space you breathe").

For Wagner the point of the scene is that the lovers *fail* to heed the watchman's warning and hence are apprehended by King Mark—an episode that leads to the love-death in Act 3. Death is an ever-present reality in Wagner's handling of the myth, as it also is in Messiaen's trilogy. A clear death-wish appears to be expressed in *Harawi*: "Coupe moi la tête" (Song 5, "L'amour de Piroutcha"); "Coupez ma tête" (Song 11, "Katchikatchi les étoiles"); and the words "La morte est là" (Song 9, "L'escalier redit, gestes du soleil") are repeated three times. Further, a cryptic but important mention of death dominates the refrain in the fifth refrain of *Cinq rechants*. Love causes anxiety, and it is recognized that it can also have fatal consequences.

But importantly in Messiaen's handling of the Tristan myth, love also has redemptive and reintegrative qualities. Joseph Kerman has noted that in Wagner's music drama the "fundamental sense is of a progress towards a state of illumination which transcends yearning and pain" and that thus, at the end, Isolde's *Liebestod* constitutes "a triumphant ascent, not a tragic catastrophe."[49] So too love is not tragic but ultimately redemptive for Messiaen, though his Tristan trilogy does not follow the strict sequential narrative pattern of the original myth. The lovers in *Harawi* pass through at least a metaphoric death and attain the status of stars that join in the cosmic dance or *lîla*. In *Turangalîla-symphonie*, the movement entitled "Joie du sang des étoiles" ("Joy of the stars' blood") engages in "excess," which demonstrates "that the union of true lovers is for them a transformation, and a transformation on a cosmic scale."[50]

12   Olivier Messiaen and the Tristan Myth

Love in the Tristan trilogy is a quality that "transcends the body, transcends even the limitations of mind, and grows to a cosmic scale."[51]

At the same time, especially in *Harawi*, which opens the trilogy, Messiaen distances the erotic story from his own personal experience and
even from the ancient Tristan story by means of grafting onto it material
from other sources, especially from the Peruvian analogue. His main
source for the Peruvian material comes from the 1925 book, *La Musique
des Incas et ses survivances*, by Raoul and Marguerite d'Harcourt.[52] While
some of the authors' interpretations and conclusions are now questioned,
especially in regard to their over-riding emphasis on pentatonicism in
ancient Peruvian music, it is nevertheless a book with which the student
of Messiaen's Tristan trilogy must come to terms. From the d'Harcourts'
book he takes the title of *Harawi*, which is derived from an important
Quechua song form, the *harawi* (later called *yaravi*, which is the more
common post-Conquest term). As set forth by the d'Harcourts, the dis-
tinguishing of genres—*harawi*, funeral lamentations, songs dealing with
the dove, dance songs, songs of farewell, etc.—involves some overlapping, and Messiaen too draws musical and textual ideas from various
of these other categories. For example, some of the *harawi*s treat the subject of the dove, an important symbol of infidelity for the Quechua-
speaking Indians. For Messiaen these songs provided a rich source of
folk material upon which he could draw as a composer. He sometimes
borrowed the actual tunes (e.g., from the *harawi* "Piruça" for Song 5,
entitled "L'amour de Piroutcha") and at other times took Quechua vocabulary, as in the case of "katchikatchi" ("grasshopper") and "toungou"
(the graceful cooing of the dove), into the fabric of his surrealistic French
verse and then into the fabric of his music.

The d'Harcourts' discussion of Peruvian folksong thus is essential to
our understanding of Messiaen's transformation of the Tristan myth, to
which he especially adds the *colombe verte* (dove) as a central image for
the Loved One. This bird, the d'Harcourts explain, is used consistently
in Quechua poetry, where it normally is associated with unhappy love
(because of the sad roulades of its song) and, as noted, with infidelity.[53]
One of the songs in the Peruvian music drama *Ollantay*, which is pre-
Conquest in origin, presents a story of two doves or pigeons, one of
which flies away, leaving its companion alone in the nest.[54] Rostand observes that Messiaen uses the equation of the *colombe verte*—a sacred bird
in folklore—with the *bien aimée*,[55] and we find this equation especially in
Song 5 of *Harawi*, where the bird is the *jeune fille* whose love call is
answered by *jeune homme*. But the remainder of the equation, *colombe
verte = bien aimée = Piroutcha* (Quechua: Piruça) = Iseult need not only

be surmised, for Messiaen himself stated that in his *Harawi* "Iseult is called Piroutcha."[56]

The utilization of folkloric materials "in music called *savante*"—i.e., learned or consciously composed music—does not occur without some difficulties, as Messiaen himself acknowledged. In his view "there are two methods of using folklore"; these include (1) "a purely *imitative method* which consists largely of utilizing known popular themes," and (2) "a *creative method* which consists, in the manner of [Manuel] de Falla or [Béla] Bartók, of creating the atmosphere of the popular music by consciously using the modes and adapted rhythms"—neither of which he admits to following.[57] Messiaen's "completely different" approach[58] was to transform melodic and rhythmic borrowings into his own modes of limited transposition and his own nonretrogradable rhythms.

Once Messiaen has cast folk materials into the mold of his musical language, the result is the retention of the melodies of the *harawi* sung in Peru while giving this Peruvian material his own personal stamp. His musical language is directly descended from Wagner and Debussy, both composers to whom he was also indebted for mythic and narrative materials. His relationship to Wagner has been frequently discussed and evaluated. For example, Arnold Whittall has noted that Messiaen "has used images of sensuality more directly than Wagner—as in 'Cinq Rechants'—but his forms have become more severely controlled."[59] Roger Smalley has written that Messiaen's "music possesses an uninhibited appetite for gargantuan emotional excess on a Wagnerian scale, and it would seem that the inspiration of Messiaen's interpretation of the Tristan legend . . . owes as much to Wagner's (*Tristan und Isolde*) as to Debussy's (*Pelléas et Mélisande*)."[60] Smalley further asserts that in Messiaen's work "the emotional scope of Wagner is wedded to a musical language derived from Debussy."[61]

The Technique of My Musical Language is replete with references to the specific traits of Debussy's style that influenced Messiaen's practice. He shows how he has taken, for example, a melodic phrase from Debussy and has used it as a "point of departure" for a new "melodic contour" in his songs "L'Épouse" and "Paysage" in *Poèmes pour Mi*, in "Combat de la mort et de la vie" in *Les Corps glorieux*, and elsewhere.[62] But more specific musical techniques have also been taken from Debussy, as in the case of "the added sixth in the perfect chord [i.e., triad], foreseen by Rameau and established by Debussy."[63] Messiaen amplified the point:

With the advent of Claude Debussy, one spoke of appoggiaturas without resolution, of passing notes with no issue, etc. In fact, one found them in his first works. In *Pelléas et Mélisande, les Estampes, les Préludes*, and *les Images* for the piano, it is a question of foreign notes, with neither preparation nor resolution, without particular expressive accent, which tranquilly make a part of the chord, changing its color, giving it a spice, a new perfume.[64]

Ultimately even Messiaen's modes of limited transposition are traceable to Debussy's use of the whole tone scale.

From the standpoint of structure, Messiaen's compositions, like Debussy's, are essentially cumulative or additive rather than developmental in the Germanic fashion. When Messiaen departed from his usual practice in order to attempt an extended development section, as in the eighth movement, "Développement de l'amour," of the *Turangalîla-symphonie,* he was splendidly successful, achieving in the latter part of the movement what one critic called "one of the most masterly things in the work."[65] Even in the earlier part of this movement, however, Messiaen relied heavily on his more usual cumulative method.[66] His way of accumulating segments takes on the unity of cyclical form—a treatment of form usually associated with César Franck, Vincent d'Indy, and their disciples.[67]

Typically, in one instance Messiaen called his work a "harmonic tapestry."[68] The metaphor is an apt description of his work in a broader sense, however, for like a tapestry it weaves together myth, poetry, and music. As ideas and images in his verses are linked together in his music, his cumulative method brings them back again and again, as in the case of the "four lizards" in the second part of *Cinq rechants*, which reappear in the fifth "movement" of the same composition. Then musically too he used linking themes that appear and reappear, as in Songs 2, 7, 9, and 12 of *Harawi*. Similarly, in *Turangalîla-symphonie*, the statue, flower, and love themes return again and again. These linkages provide a degree of unity or coherence to his compositions.

Another technical device that functions to promote coherence in *Harawi* and *Turangalîla-symphonie*, but almost not at all in *Cinq rechants*, is Messiaen's way of linking chords through a common tone in a long series of either ascending or descending passages. I prefer to call this device *enchainment*, since no ready-made term seems to fit Messiaen's practice of utilizing the device with such great persistency and regularity. I derive this term from a hint in his own poetry, which uses the words *enchaînée* and *chaînes* as part of an important pattern of imagery in *Harawi* (Songs 2, 5, 10).

The Composer and the Myth 15

What, then, is the total aesthetic effect of Messiaen's musical language as he used it in the Tristan trilogy and elsewhere? His rhythmic practice is crucial here. As David Drew noted, his added time values are "destructive . . . of a regular pulse."[69] Listening to Messiaen's asymmetrical rhythms is often like waiting for a second shoe to drop. His nonretrogradable rhythms also have a static quality, since something that can be run backward as well as forward can be construed as actually circular in form. Furthermore, the absence of bar lines as well as the ever-changing number of beats in a measure will destroy the regular progression of a piece. For Messiaen, true *rhythm* means a complex and irregular pattern opposed to march time, and thus he criticizes Johann Sebastian Bach as having "no rhythm" on account of his regularity.[70] Hence one of the most significant elements to be examined in any study of the effects of Messiaen's Tristan trilogy or of any of his other works must be his approach to time. His rhythms were not devised without purpose. Through the destruction of conventional rhythmic practices he aimed to create a sense of timelessness.[71]

To achieve this effect, Messiaen looked back at plainchant rhythms and Greek metrics, but he also was influenced by the ametricism of Igor Stravinsky. Further, he found himself influenced by the North Indian rhythms (*talas*) of the thirteenth-century theorist Śarṅgadeva.[72] Messiaen said that he was aided initially in his understanding of the 120 *deçi-talas* by a Hindu friend, who elucidated the Sanskrit symbols.[73] Three of the *talas* were noted by him with particular affection:[74]

simhavikrîdita:

rāgavardhana:

gajalîla:

Actual Indian rhythms not only were taken into his compositions, but also were the basis for the transformation of his entire rhythmic language. Additive rather than divisive, Indian rhythms gave him the impetus for the idea of added time values, and from the rhythm of the *rāgavardhana tala* he derived rhythms that are identical in both forward and retrograde form. For example, in the body of the first movement of *Turangalîla-symphonie* he used the retrograde form of this *tala* as the rhythmic pattern for the violins and violas; the pattern, repeated thirteen and one-half times, is woven into the fabric of four other rhythmic schemes in the woodwinds, brass, gamelan (consisting of vibraphone, celesta, and keyed glockenspiel), and percussion, respectively. The effect, therefore, is a static, nonprogressing rhythm, as if reaching outside of time itself.

In contrast, then, to the tradition of Western music since the early baroque monodists who established the practice of capitalizing on driving rhythms, Messiaen rejected any such utilization of forward-pressing motion or desire to progress in music. The late sixteenth and seventeenth centuries marked a basic change in man's orientation toward time, which became an obsession not only for musicians but also for philosophers, scientists, and merchants.[75] Time came to mean generally a sense of urgency—a sense of urgency that seems even demonic, as may be indicated by the change in iconography: Time in the sixteenth century becomes no longer a benign figure, but a sinister destroyer.[76] Messiaen, himself a man who was constantly working and never allowed himself to take a holiday, recognized the pressure of modern urban life with its intense time consciousness.[77] He was not interested merely in escape from unpleasant reality; in his music, which consciously reverts to nature as found in bird songs and which usually eschews the kind of fundamental drive that builds toward a conclusion, he seriously attempted to achieve a legitimate freedom from the tyranny of time.

The effect of Messiaen's music in the Tristan trilogy thus has been usefully contrasted with Beethoven. Drew, for example, observes that the opening of the C major piano sonata (Opus 53) of Beethoven "is the accumulation of tension throughout an immense anacrusis, which culminates in the shift to the dominant's dominant in the last quarter of the second bar, is consummated with the arrival at the dominant, and then released in two stages. The nature of this event is such that at the recurrence of the idea a new, interacting, experience is dramatically imperative, rather than a repetition of the old."[78] In contrast, Drew notes that the works of Messiaen, like those of Stravinsky, "give rise to tensions, but this is an extraneous and purely physical effect of something that is without tendency, something that involves no idea of 'becoming' but merely observes the behaviour in space of certain objects or cellules. . . . With Beethoven it is what *happens* that matters; Stravinsky and Messiaen are merely concerned with what *is*."[79]

By rejecting the modern pressure of time, Messiaen is in a way returning to an essentially medieval sense of the temporal, which held that time is contained within eternity and is dependent on God at every mo-

The Composer and the Myth 17

ment.[80] There is tension in his music, of course, but it is the tension that is encountered in the structure of things and in the condition of life. Such tension does not need to be generated or worked up in the manner of Beethoven. This fact has immense significance for Messiaen's work, for he was thus able in his composition to express at once his own indignation at the modern conception of time and also to create a music that takes the listener into a realm of the imagination beyond the usual considerations of time as he or she encounters them in the workaday world. "Time," he said in 1971, by contrast "makes Eternity comprehensible to us."[81] Listeners at performances of his works as a general rule have reacted intensely, and those who have become caught up in this music have experienced it much more intensely than most traditional Western music. His music thus has much in common with more recent composers such as Henryk Górecki, Arvo Pärt, Zbigniew Preisner, and John Tavener, who like Messiaen have also tended to turn to religious themes.

Messiaen's musical language hence involves a revolt against "arbitrary regularity" in rhythm[82]—a regularity that is dominated by chronological time (or at least by the metronome). Generally time is regarded mechanistically, as something measurable, but, as Pierrette Mari notes, for Messiaen time was "a notion essentially relative"—a notion that takes into account not the clock or metronome but "the insect, the mountain, or the galaxy." Mari continues: "It is necessary [for Messiaen] to abolish material time in order to descend into interior timelessness. . . . All his works constitute a research into pure interior time and a dramatic attempt to mediate between time and eternity. . . . One sees that for him rhythm has a significance equal to (if not more important than) duration for Bergson."[83] Significantly, for Bergson too, time and music stand in a special relationship. "A melody to which we listen with our eyes closed, heeding it alone," he wrote, "comes very close to coinciding with this time which is the very *fluidity of our inner life*."[84]

In each of the three works in the Tristan trilogy, Messiaen's preoccupation with the problem of time is explicitly evident. In Song 9 ("L'escalier redit, gestes du soleil") of *Harawi*, for example, he juxtaposes time, water, and heaven—a triad of associations, which is indicative of the relationship between time and nature and between time and the eternal. The word *turanga* in the title of *Turangalîla-symphonie* means "time which runs like a galloping horse; . . . time that flows, like sand in an hourglass,"[85] but here again the musical treatment has the effect of abolishing the regularity of the inexorable passage of time. This treatment of musical material is extended into *Cinq rechants*, which combines a very

18   Olivier Messiaen and the Tristan Myth

fragmented text with a setting that alternates passages of more and less irregularity.

Messiaen seemed to know that his mythic material, drawn from the Tristan and Iseult story, needed to be understood within the context of time, in which human life moves and has its being, often oblivious of the eternity that he believed sustained the temporal. In other accounts, the myth involves the death of the lovers just as the culmination of life itself comes with the end of life. However, as they live in Messiaen's music in a kind of cosmic space, the lovers manage to transcend ordinary time and even ordinary death.

NOTES

1. See the surveys by Thomas Kerth, "Legend of Tristan," and Guy Mermier, "Roman de Tristan," in *The Dictionary of the Middle Ages*, 13 vols. (New York: Scribners, 1984–89), 12: 199–203.

2. "Interview with Yvonne Loriod," in Peter Hill, ed., *The Messiaen Companion* (London: Faber and Faber, 1994), 303.

3. See *Olivier Messiaen: A Bibliographical Catalogue of Messiaen's Works* (Tutzing: Hans Schneider, 1998), 93. The first performances were in June 1946, with the soprano Marcelle Bunlet accompanied by the composer.

4. Olivier Messiaen, *Music and Color: Conversations with Claude Samuel*, trans. E. Thomas Glasgow (Portland, Oregon: Amadeus Press, 1994), 129; these interviews include material from Claude Samuel, *Entretiens avec Olivier Messiaen* (Paris: Belfond, 1967), as well as later additions.

5. See "Interview with Yvonne Loriod," 294–95.

6. See Paul Griffiths, "*Saint François d'Assise*," in Hill, ed., *The Messiaen Companion*, 488–509; and Nils Holger Petersen, "Messiaen's *Saint François d'Assise* and Franciscan Spirituality," in Siglind Bruhn, ed., *Messiaen's Language of Mystical Love* (New York: Garland, 1998), 169–93.

7. Messiaen, *Music and Color*, 20.

8. Olivier Messiaen, "Address Delivered at the Conferring of the Praemium Erasmianum on June 25, 1971," in Almut Rössler, *Contributions to the Spiritual World of Oliver Messiaen, with Original Texts by the Composer*, trans. Barbara Dagg and Nancy Poland (Duisburg: Gilles and Francke, 1986), 39.

9. Olivier Messiaen, Address at Conférence de Notre Dame, 4 December 1977, in Rössler, *Contributions*, 65.

10. Olivier Messiaen, Préface, *Quatour pour la fin du temps* (Paris: Durand, 1942), i.

11. Ibid., i–ii. Here Messiaen describes his way of hearing colors and seeing chords and melodies. In "gyrations of superhuman sounds and colors," he perceives "daggers of *fire*, torrents of blue-orange lava, sharp-pointed stars." See also Jonathan W. Bernard, "Messiaen's Synaesthesia: The Correspondence between Color and Sound in His Music," *Music Perception* 4 (1986): 41–68.

12. Olivier Messiaen, *Poèmes pour Mi* (Paris: Durand, 1939).

The Composer and the Myth 19

13. Rodin Museum, Paris.

14. Messiaen, *Poèmes pour Mi*, 1: 12–15.

15. Antoine Goléa, *Rencontres avec Olivier Messiaen* (Paris: Julliard, 1960), 130; translations from this work and other works where no translator is indicated are mine.

16. Olivier Messiaen, *The Technique of My Musical Language*, trans. John Satterfield, 2 vols. (Paris: Alphonse Leduc, 1956), 1: 71.

17. Guy Ferchault, "De la Mort de Frank à nos jours," in *La Revue musicale* (La Musique religieuse française), as quoted in Stuart Waumsley, *The Organ Music of Olivier Messiaen*, 2nd ed. (Paris: Leduc, 1975), 9 (italics added).

18. Samuel, *Entretiens*, 19.

19. Tanneguy de Quénetain, "Messiaen, Poet of Nature," *Music and Musicians* 11 (May 1963): 9–10.

20. Messiaen, *Music and Color*, 31.

21. Ibid., 20–21 (italics added).

22. Quoted by de Quénetain, "Messiaen, Poet of Nature," 10.

23. See Joseph L. Henderson, "Ancient Myths and Modern Man," in *Man and His Symbols*, ed. Carl G. Jung (Garden City, N.Y.: Doubleday, 1964), 152–53.

24. "Hommage," l. 13, in Stéphane Mallarmé, *Selected Poems*, ed. C. F. MacIntyre (Berkeley and Los Angeles: University of California Press, 1965), 94.

25. See also Larry W. Peterson, "Messiaen and Surrealism: A Study of His Poetry," in *Messiaen's Language of Mystical Love*, ed. Bruhn, 215–24.

26. Nahma Sandrow, *Surrealism: Theatre, Arts, Ideas* (New York: Harper and Row, 1972), 61–62.

27. Olivier Messiaen, *Cinq rechants* (Paris: Editions Salabert, 1949), 3.

28. See Paul Griffiths, *Olivier Messiaen and the Music of Time* (Ithaca: Cornell University Press, 1985), 127–28.

29. Pierrette Mari, *Olivier Messiaen* (Paris: Seghers, 1965), 64.

30. Bernard Gavoty and Olivier Messiaen, "Who Are You, Olivier Messiaen?" *Tempo* 58 (Summer 1961): 36.

31. See de Quénetain, "Messiaen, Poet of Nature," 8.

32. Quoted by Geoffrey Brereton, *An Introduction to French Poets* (Fair Lawn, N.J.: Essential Books, 1957), 204; and quoted in turn by Roger Smalley, "Debussy and Messiaen," *Musical Times* 109 (1968): 130.

33. Edward Lockspeiser, *Debussy: His Life and Mind*, 2 vols. (New York: Macmillan, 1962), 1:152; quoted by Smalley, "Debussy and Messiaen," 129.

34. See William S. Rubin, *Dada, Surrealism, and Their Heritage* (New York: Museum of Modern Art, 1968), 106; Werner Spies and Helmut Rudolf Leppien, *Max Ernst Oeuvre-Katalog*, 3 vols. (Cologne: DuMont Schauberg, 1975), no. 1563.

35. Sandrow, *Surrealism*, 21.

36. Ibid., 21.

37. Mari, *Olivier Messiaen*, 46. For Messiaen's way of working on texts and music, see "Interview with Yvonne Loriod," 285–86.

38. Quoted in Mari, *Olivier Messiaen*, 5; translated as "The blonde hair on the bulging forehead, eyes of hazel, eyes smiling, singing, thinking, a little droll square nose, a beautiful, playful dimple."

20 Olivier Messiaen and the Tristan Myth

39. Heinz Werner Zimmermann, "Ein Gespräch mit Olivier Messiaen," *Musik und Kirche* 39 (1969): 39.

40. This observation is influenced by structuralist anthropology; see Claude Lévi-Strauss, *The Raw and the Cooked*, trans. John and Doreen Weightman (New York: Harper and Row, 1969), 14–15.

41. Ibid., 15.

42. See Messiaen, *Music and Color*, 30.

43. Cf. ibid., 30, for Messiaen's disavowal of any connection with either the ancient Celtic legend or with the episode of the love potion, except for a few allusions in *Cinq rechants*. The "philtre à deux voix" refers to the love potion that can also bring death. But see also *Harawi*, Songs 7 and 9.

44. Mari, *Olivier Messiaen*, 52.

45. Translations from Wagner's text are mine; for the music accompanying this scene, see *Tristan und Isolde*, ed. Isolde Vetter, Sämtliche Werke 8, pts. 1–3 (Mainz: B. Schott's Söhne, 1990), 2: 143–44.

46. Goléa, *Rencontres*, 158.

47. For the music accompanying this scene, see Wagner, *Tristan und Isolde*, ed. Vetter, 1: 162–63.

48. Song 8 ("Syllabes"); see also Claude Rostand, *Olivier Messiaen* (Paris: Ventadour, 1957), 36, who refers to the "Danse des Singes."

49. Joseph Kerman, *Opera as Drama*, revised ed. (Berkeley and Los Angeles: University of California Press, 1988), 160.

50. Olivier Messiaen, Program notes accompanying recording of *Turangalîla-Symphonie* (Deutsche Grammophon 431 781–2), 5.

51. Messiaen, *Music and Color*, 30.

52. Raoul d'Harcourt and Marguerite d'Harcourt, *La Musique des Incas et ses survivances*, 2 vols. (Paris: Paul Geuthner, 1925).

53. Ibid., 1:190. The words "colombe verte" have the connotation of "loved one" in French. For emphasizing this point I am indebted to Robert Laudon.

54. D'Harcourt and d'Harcourt, *La Musique des Incas*, 1: 190.

55. Rostand, *Olivier Messiaen*, 35–36.

56. Goléa, *Rencontres*, 150.

57. Ibid., 149 (italics added).

58. Ibid.

59. Arnold Whittall, "Stravinsky and Music Drama," *Music and Letters* 50 (1969): 66. Whittall contrasts the anti-Romantic Stravinsky and the Romantic Messiaen: "Messiaen's rituals spring from an *acceptance* of the world" (italics added).

60. Smalley, "Debussy and Messiaen," 128. As has been frequently noted, Messiaen has seen the story of *Pelléas et Mélisande* as an analogue to the Tristan story and may have incorporated some details from the dialogue of Debussy's opera, for which Maeterlinck provided the libretto. For example, in Act 3, scene 1, of *Pelléas et Mélisande*, the beautiful long hair of Mélisande falls from the window and entangles Pelléas in its locks, and just at that moment two doves—the birds of Venus in medieval secular iconography—fly about the tower. The falling hair is echoed in *Harawi*, where in Song 10 ("Amour oiseau d'étoile") the head is reversed under the heavens and the hands reach up to touch the entangling hair. The dove, which appears as the *colombe verte* from Peruvian folklore, also has a

long history as an erotic symbol in the West. In medieval illustrations in manuscripts of the *Roman de la Rose*, doves form the team that draws the vehicle in which Venus rides.

61. Smalley, "Debussy and Messiaen," 128.

62. Messiaen, *The Technique of My Musical Language*, 1: 32; vol. 2, exs. 85–89. Cf. Smalley, "Debussy and Messiaen," 128. On Debussy's use of melody, see Martin Cooper, *French Music from the Death of Berlioz to the Death of Fauré* (London: Oxford University Press, 1951), 97.

63. Messiaen, *The Technique of My Musical Language*, 1: 31.

64. Ibid., 1: 47.

65. David Drew, "Messiaen—A Provisional Study (III)," *The Score and I.M.A. Magazine*, no. 14 (Dec. 1955): 55.

66. See ibid., 55, for Drew's complaint: "Nor is there much to be said in favour of the tedious repetitive pattern of the first part of the eighth movement. . . ." See also the discussion of the eighth movement of the symphony in Leonard Burkat, "Current Chronicle," *Musical Quarterly* 36 (1950): 265–66.

67. Cooper, *French Music*, 48.

68. Messiaen, *The Technique of My Musical Language*, 1: 39.

69. Drew, "Messiaen—A Provisional Study (II)," *The Score and I.M.A. Magazine*, no. 13 (September 1955): 65.

70. Messiaen, *Music and Color*, 68.

71. See Antoine Goléa, "Das Weltbild des Komponisten Olivier Messiaen," *Neue Zeitschrift für Musik* 130 (1969): 22; cf. Drew, "Messiaen—A Provisional Study (III)," 51.

72. See Joanny Grosset, "Histoire de la musique: Inde," in *Encyclopédie de la musique et dictionnaire du conservatoire*, ed. A. Lavignac (Paris: Delagrave, 1913–31), vol. 1, pt. 1, esp. pp. 287–324.

73. Messiaen, *Music and Color*, 75–77.

74. Messiaen, *The Technique of My Musical Language*, vol. 2, exs. 2–3; Śarṅgadeva as cited by Grosset, "Histoire de la musique: Inde," 301, 303; see also Messiaen, *Music and Color*, 77–78.

75. See Ricardo Quinones, *The Renaissance Discovery of Time* (Cambridge: Harvard University Press, 1972), 3–27.

76. Erwin Panofsky, *Studies in Iconology* (1939; reprint New York: Harper and Row, 1962), 69–94.

77. "Interview with Yvonne Loriod," 283–84.

78. Drew, "Messiaen—A Provisional Study (II)," 68.

79. Ibid., 68–69.

80. See Victor Zuckerkandl, *Sound and Symbol*, trans. Willard Trask, Bollingen Series, 44 (1956; reprint Princeton: Princeton University Press, 1969), 155–56.

81. Messiaen, "Address Delivered at the Conferring of the Praemium Erasmianum," in Rössler, *Contributions*, 40. See also the sentence from St. Thomas Aquinas at the opening of Messiaen's *Traité de rythme*, as quoted in translation (from the *Summa Theologiae*, trans. Timothy McDermott [London: Eyre and Spottiswood, 1964], 2: 101) by Jean Boivin, "Messiaen's Teaching at the Paris Conservatoire: A Humanist's Legacy," in *Messiaen's Language of Mystical Love*, ed. Bruhn, 15: "Time measures not only what is effectively changing, but what is

changeable: hence it measures not just motion, but also rest; the state of a being born to move yet not presently moving."

82. Mari, *Olivier Messiaen*, 57.

83. Ibid.

84. Henri Bergson, *Duration and Simultaneity*, trans. Leon Jacobson, 2nd ed. (London: Clinamen Press, 1999), 30 (italics added). See also Zuckerkandl, *Sound and Symbol*, 141.

85. Messiaen, Notes accompanying recording of *Turangalîla-Symphonie* (DGG 431 781–2), 1.

2

Harawi: Song of Love and Death

The twelve songs of Messiaen's song cycle *Harawi: Chant d'amour et de mort*,[1] scored for a solo woman's voice (Messiaen specified that it should be a "large, dramatic soprano voice"[2]) and piano, are immensely demanding for the performers both technically and in the presentation of mood. The song texts, following the tradition of the romantic *Lied* and modern French song, give to a woman's voice even those verses that would logically seem more appropriate for a man to sing, as in a section labelled "le jeune homme" in Song 5 ("L'amour de Piroutcha"),[3] yet a form of dialogue is preserved in another and unique manner between the pianist and the female voice. Like the later *Turangalîla-symphonie*, *Harawi* fluctuates in mood between light and darkness but never achieves the degree of joyful expression and psychological release that will be present in the symphony. Mountains, an important source of strength to Messiaen in his childhood, also are identified with something terrifying and ambiguous in Song 3 ("Montagnes"), where paradoxically they provide a symbolic landscape for deep anguish as the lover stands dizzily over the abyss of despair and fear. However, Song 4 ("Doundou tchil") shows a recovery in which despair is overcome by the image of the rainbow and by the glance of the loved one. The lovers are caught in the Staircase of Time in Song 9 ("L'escalier redit, gestes du soleil"), yet in the tenth song ("Amour oiseau d'étoile") they are able to rise above time. The imprisonment of the lovers as well as their final apotheosis in *Harawi* will also return in *Cinq rechants*, where they are encapsulated and trapped in the crystal ball (borrowed from Bosch's *The Garden of Earthly Delights*) and then are able to fly away finally to freedom.

In the shaping of *Harawi*, Messiaen borrowed and transformed fragmented images from Wagner's *Tristan und Isolde*, from the Peruvian analogue to the Tristan story, and from a common stock of Surrealist imagery. Thus in Song 1 ("La ville qui dormait toi") there are not only the bank and glances of the lovers out of Act 2 of Wagner's opera, but also images of heart, hand, and eye, the latter two being ubiquitous in Surrealist painting. In Song 4 ("Doundou tchil") the sound of ankle bells from Peruvian folk music dances is joined to images of stars, birds, rainbow, and fruit. Yet the result is remarkably coherent, held together by the composer's use of such musical material as Peruvian folk melodies, which he found exceedingly beautiful—musical material that he transformed and adapted to his modes of limited transposition.[4]

While Messiaen provided no divisions in the twelve-song cycle, the texts seem to fall into three sections. Songs 1 through 4 trace the fluctuation of mood and scene from a seemingly idyllic setting while the town sleeps, through premonition of separation at morning and an experience of dizziness, until a return to an integrated psychological state is indicated by a dance song. The pattern is descent and recovery—a pattern that represents for the composer the shape of the abyss on the edge of which the *persona* of the poetic text balances. In Songs 5 through 9, the texts and music both display a great deal of tension. There seems to be little sense of order here except that they dramatize an unsuccessful striving for integration. Even more than in other parts of the cycle, the images and verses seem to come apart, displaying a personal and psychological turmoil. The culmination is in Song 9, which forms the point analogous to the crisis in the well-made play. The emphasis in the images is on death, either the actual physical death of the lovers or their terror of death (physical and spiritual) as something that must be lived through. Or do the references to death point to an ecstasy at once physical and mystical?

The mood changes in the final three songs of the cycle ("Amour oiseau d'étoile," "Katchikatchi les étoiles," and "Dans le noir"), for here the experience of love appears ultimately to be ennobling for those who have encountered it. Yet death is not simply put aside, for here it is as if the lovers have died and now grandly attain their apotheosis. The final song recapitulates images, phrases, and melodic material from earlier songs as a way of emphasizing this achievement. Remarkably the seemingly disjunctive images and melodic phrases are brought together in a kind of wholeness as the cycle concludes. The impression is of unity as well as of a wonderful diversity.

PART I

Song I

"La ville qui dormait, toi" provides a point of reference throughout the rest of the cycle. The text may be translated as follows.[5]

The town which slept, you.
My hand on your heart by you.
The heart of midnight, the bank, you.
The double of the violet, you.
The eye immobile, without unraveling your look, me.

Here, in the countryside, while the town sleeps at "le plein minuit," the lovers are together. The lover looks at his beloved in the pleasure of the moment—a moment, as in the medieval *alba*, that he must know cannot be infinitely extended. As noted, the bank on which they recline is a detail suggested by Wagner's *Tristan und Isolde*, and the deep of the night is also the time when Pelléas and Mélisande were discovered together in Debussy's opera, the score of which the composer had known since he was a boy of ten.[6] The introduction of a flower with a specific color, "La violette double," requires a new symbolic level, however, for here the personal and universal come together, at least in the composer's interpretation. The color violet, when it has more red in it, was said by Messiaen to be traditionally symbolic of the Truth of Love, while when it tended toward blue, it symbolized the Love of Truth;[7] expressed in music, the latter is his Mode 2. He must also have known that violet is a symbol of affliction, as when used as a liturgical color in vestments. In the song the color, whatever its intended meaning, is consistent with the knowledge that love can bring pain as well as joy. Affliction, absent from "La ville qui dormait, toi," will appear soon enough in the next song when the day comes and the lovers must part.

The music of Song 1 deserves careful attention and analysis. In shape, it extends to the use of *pianissimo* (*ppp*) at the beginning and builds to a controlled climax at *mezzo forte* (*mf*) just past its center, then returns to an even softer *pianissimo* (*pppp*) at the end. The first line is sung on a single note, D, repeated five times until there is a leap to the last note, B, which ends the phrase. The D–B interval and its chordal accompaniment outline the G major tonality. The five-line text is then shaped into a six-phrase musical structure that possesses theme, middle period, and final period.[8] The final period is characterized by Messiaen's principle of development by elimination, as the words "sans denouer ton regard, moi" are set to truncated portions of earlier themes. But his style here is not so much dependent on the building of climaxes as it is a movement that does not need to arrive at any predetermined conclusion. Each chord is enchained with every other chord. Resolution may be held back by a delicious delay of an added rhythmic value on an almost embarrassingly sweet chord—a chord that could have had its origin in the vocabulary of jazz sounds—after which the resolution can take place on a chord (the added sixth on the tonic) that should sound even more suspiciously sweet to our ears but that, in the composer's hands, is made to seem exactly right. Messiaen, who composed his text and music at the same time (unlike Wagner or, for that matter, most composers whose texts were written long before they were set to music), was a master of *mood*.

The song's last two words, "regard, moi," are separated carefully from what has gone before by a breathing mark; thus they may be regarded as a unit, in this case set to the melodic interval of an ascending augmented fourth, followed by a descending major seventh with the note D and its final chord resolving into the G major tonality. The augmented fourth that appears previous to the resolution is an example of the tritone that appears over and over again in Messiaen's works, both in the compositions preceding the Tristan trilogy and in the trilogy itself. It emerges (as a melodic interval of either an augmented fourth, as here, or as a diminished fifth) three times in the short span of this song. Wilfrid Mellers has commented on both Wagner's and Messiaen's predilection for the tritone, which in the Middle Ages was understood to represent the devil ("si contra fa diabolus est").[9] For Wagner, combinations of perfect, diminished, and augmented fourths represented a "burden of consciousness, sensuality, frustrated aspiration, and guilt," as Mellers notes.[10] Messiaen's use of the *si contra fa* is less codified and more spiritual than in Wagner, and in his religious works it appears to be more often for him associated with angels and their representatives, the birds, than with guilt. In *Harawi*, however, the tritone is more ambiguous, since these are songs of love and death outside the frame of religious rite and belief.

Harawi: Song of Love and Death 27

Perhaps the tritone is Messiaen's symbol of acceptance of human as well as earthly love—or of his realization that these are intimately linked to spiritual love.

Song 2

In "Bonjour toi, colombe verte" the time is no longer "the heart of midnight." Day has come. Unlike Wagner's treatment of the story or the traditional *alba*, there has been no warning of approaching danger or daylight. This element will not appear until Song 8 ("Syllables"), during which the *alba* will be transformed into the warning cry of the monkeys: "pia, pia, pia." But the day does mean separation for the lovers which is represented in Messiaen's verse in fractured and surrealistic images, addressed to the green dove (*colombe verte*) of Quechua folklore.[11]

> Good day to you, green dove,
> Returned from the heaven.
> Good day to you, limpid pearl,
> Departure of the water.
> Star-linked,
> Shadow-sharing,
> You, of flower, of fruit,
> Of heaven and water,
> Song of birds.
> Good day, Water.

In the musical setting, a six-tone tune from Peruvian folk music—"Delirio," which is a melody that serves almost as the "theme" for the entire cycle—is introduced, but not in its original form (that is, as a tune in the key of E♭ major).[12] For the melody, the second tone is raised from a major second to an augmented second, as in Example 2.1. Messiaen has here transformed the tune "Delirio" into a melody that is not strictly major or modal, though the tones of the song are used in such a way as to suggest his modal combination of minor and augmented thirds, half steps, and an ascending diminished fifth. The musical material from "Delirio" is thus changed in the prism of the composer's musical language, as it will also be in Songs 7 ("Adieu"), 9 ("L'escalier redit"), and 12 ("Dans le noir"). Each phrase of text and music in "Bonjour toi, colombe verte" is accompanied and followed by cascades of rippling thirty-second notes at a fast tempo and a high *tessitura* representing the bird

Example 2.1

DELIRIO

BONJOUR TOI, COLOMBE VERTE

songs (because in nature birds sing very high and fast). Bird songs are, of course, very familiar elsewhere in Messiaen's works, most notably perhaps in *Catalogue d'Oiseaux*. When the melody changes to one consisting of a descending diminished fifth, a kind of inversion of the first melody, the accompaniment follows in sevenths, fourths, and thirds of varying sizes.

The representation of the beloved in terms of the *colombe verte*, the green dove which deserts its mate in Peruvian folklore,[13] is a sign that Messiaen is specifically thinking of the unfaithful heroine in the Tristan story. But the symbolism is extremely mixed and ambiguous. Like Iseult, the bird is unfaithful, but it is also very affectionate; in Peruvian folklore, she deserts her mate and yet is associated with tender love. For Messiaen, she becomes even the beneficent "Chant des oiseaux"—the song set apart from the bird itself. The symbolism is even more ambiguous when examined in the light of Western iconography, for which the dove, originally sacred to Aphrodite, became transformed into the emblem of chastity and peace—and even into a symbol of the Holy Spirit.[14] But there can be no doubt that for Messiaen in *Harawi* the bird was somehow a creature that is to be seen as symbolic of transcendence. It will come as no surprise to learn that for some primitive cultures birds are "the 'messengers' of the celestial spirits."[15] The composer, an enthusiastic collector of bird songs, used them in his compositions for their symbolic value as well as for their beauty. The color green is also important, for green is traditionally associated with spring, a time of year sacred to Venus. The images of fruit, flowers, heaven, and water suggest that for Messiaen we have here symbols representing the provider of all good

Harawi: Song of Love and Death   29

things. Another element is introduced in the "perle limpide" ("limpid pearl") and in the image of water—the latter image previously used by the composer in a spiritual sense as "the water of grace" in *Les Corps glorieux*, written for the organ in 1939. There is in the song "Bonjour toi, colombe verte" an almost mystical sense in the way he apprehends the beloved, who is also designated as "star-linked" ("Étoile en chaîne"), for she clearly functions for him as one who brings light and life. The "departure of water" ("Départ de l'eau") will leave him apart from the woman who has become the center of his existence, a condition perhaps indicated by the way the final words of the song are accompanied by a repetition of descending sevenths, fourths, and thirds in addition to a group of sixths and fifths, which provide a basis for rounding out the piece. As the voice holds out the final tone, the piano closes the section with descending chords based on the tonic.

Song 3

In sharp contrast to the preceding songs is "Montagnes," where the colors identified in the text are red-violet and extreme blackness ("Rouge violet, noir sur noir") and the mountain is invoked to "listen to the solar confusion of dizziness" ("écoute le chaos solaire du vertige," the final word of which is emphasized in the vocal line by an upward leap) while "la pierre agenouillée porte ses maîtres noir" ("the genuflecting stone carries its black masters").

> Violet-red, black on black.
> The antiquated, useless ray of black,
> Mountain, listen to the solar confusion of dizziness.
> The genuflecting stone carries its black masters.
> In tight hoods the spruces hasten toward the black.
> The abyss, thrown everywhere into dizziness.
> Black on black.

The imagery suggests the strong conflict of conscience and desire, which are represented in this poem by blackness and the abyss, the latter, to be sure, always an ambiguous symbol in Messiaen's work. In his *Livre d'Orgue* (1951) he identified two abysses, one of human misery (*la misère humaine*) and another of divine grace (*la misericorde divine*),[16] both of them associated with dizziness and both bottomless. But in his *Quatuor pour la fin du temps* Messiaen had identified the abyss with "time, with its sadness, its lassitudes" and positioned it as the opposite of the birds, who represent "our desire for light, for the stars, for rainbows and jubilant songs."[17] The important thing here is the interrelationship of time, despair, the abyss, and birds, which are the agents by which hope is brought. But in this song the despair seems overwhelming. The *très vif* sections, written for piano alone, are agitated and nervous; they are characterized by harmonies with two polytonal chords that rock back and forth. At the direction *modéré* the enlarged chords come crashing down to lead into the vocal part, which is low and menacing. The voice achieves a kind of *parlando*, followed by the large chords in a descending pattern. The third phrase of the text "Montagne, écoute le chaos..." begins with the low *parlando* but moves upward to a long-held note on c♯ on which the singer crescendoes. The text sets the mood. The chasm throws everything into vertigo: "Gouffre lancé partout dans le vertige." Long passages of chords made up of eighth notes, sixteenth notes of various kinds (some dotted), and the final descending thirty-second-note arpeggios precede the last despairing "noir sur noir" ("black on black").

In the verse the mountains nevertheless seem to be standing aloof from the despair and anxiety expressed in this song. The *persona* addresses the mountains, which here would appear to be the Andes in keeping with the other Peruvian lore in the cycle, though the composer had not yet seen them at the time when he wrote *Harawi*. Paradoxically, mountains and birds represent stability and comprise a counter-image to the chaos and the abyss. The blackness that surrounds the speaker is despair and a feeling of uselessness, both apparently very real to the composer:

> In dark hours, when my *uselessness* is brutally revealed to me and all the musical languages of the world seem to be merely an effort of patient research, without there being anything behind the notes to justify so much work—I go into the forest, into fields, into *mountains*, by the sea, among birds.... [I]t is there that music dwells for me; free, anonymous, improvised for pleasure.[18]

Even in this song there are glimmers of hope opposed to the blackness, as the presence of violet-red, standing for the Truth of Love in Messiaen's understanding of color, had suggested in the first line of its text.

Song 4

"Doundou tchil" is a dance song that functions as a point of recovery after the anguished invoking of the abyss in the previous song. Furthermore, it provides a joyous closure to the first unit of four songs.

> Doundou tchil [repeated].
> Piroutcha, here you are,
> Dance of the stars, doundou tchil.
> Piroutcha, there you are,
> Mirror of familiar birds, doundou tchil.
> Rainbow, my breath, my echo,
> Your glance has returned, tchil.
> Piroutcha, you are here,
> My buoyant fruit in the light, doundou tchil.
> Toungou, mapa, nama, mapa, kahipipas.
> Toungou, mapa, nama, mapa, mahipipas.

The opening words are borrowings from Quechua: "Doundou tchil," an onomatopoetic expression for the sounds made by the ankle bells of dancers, sung forty-eight times on one tone (C$\sharp$ to a regularly recurring rhythmic pattern (two sixteenth notes followed by an eighth), with each repetition of the word followed by two quarter-note rests. This is accompanied by bell-like sixteenth- and thirty-second notes only in the left hand, graced by acciacaturas. At the repetition of the "doundou tchil" pattern, the left hand is joined by the right hand playing bird-song melodies. The sound is like Indian ankle bells with kanjira accompaniment, and it is safe to say that the composer was consciously blending techniques from the music of India with Quechua song.

The source of the words "doundou tchil" is the dance song "Quisiera, quisiera ser danzantito" that Messiaen had found in the d'Harcourt collection, where it is identified as a piece to be sung during "the Festival of the God; it accompanies untiringly the choreographic 'sports' of the dancers dressed in a carnival fashion, and who have cloth or leather leggings . . . which are decorated with dangling bells that ring with each movement"[19] (Example 2.2). The text of this Quechua song invokes the bells:

> I would like to be a noble dancer
> With ankle bells on my feet,

Example 2.2

Doundou tchil, tchil-tchil-tchil!
In order to dance with my betrothed
From now until the dawn.
Doundou tchil, tchil-tchil-tchil!

Messiaen used this dance as his inspiration in creating a very different dance of joy that celebrates the spiritual union of the lovers. Consider the fifth movement of *Turangalîla-symphonie*, which dramatizes, as the composer himself noted, the joining together of the lovers as a "transformation" of cosmic dimensions.[20] In Song 4 of *Harawi* the dance is a "transformation" that is an integrative experience linking the lovers to the very order of the cosmos. Thus there is a connection with the cosmic dance, with the Hindu idea of *lîla*, with the planets whirling and stars jumping like grasshoppers, as in "Katchikatchi les étoiles," the eleventh song of the cycle. In Song 4 the beloved is identified as the "dance of the stars."

The recovery is brought about by the return of the beloved, now for the first time called by her Peruvian name, Piroutcha, after the character in Quechua song that the composer also was to use as the source for a tune in Song 5 ("L'amour de Piroutcha"). In Song 4, Piroutcha is the mirror image of familiar birds, which, as we have seen, are symbolic of rescue from the abyss. She is bird and rainbow—another image that mediates between earth and heaven, especially in Scandinavian mythology, where it was thought to be a bridge built by the gods between heaven and earth.[21] In Christian iconography, the rainbow is a symbol of hope and a sign of pardon—i.e., of divine intervention promised in order to bridge the abyss that separates fallen man from God.[22] Messiaen's fondness for rainbows and the analogies he draws between sounds and the rainbow's colors are well known. He says in his *Technique of My Musical Language*: "My secret desire of enchanted gorgeousness in harmony has pushed me toward those swords of fire, those sudden stars, those flows of blue-orange lavas, those planets of turquoise, those violet shades, those garnets of long-haired arborescence, those wheelings of sounds and colors in a jumble of rainbows of which I have spoken with love in the Preface of my *Quatuor pour la fin du Temps*."[23] Rainbows thus had for him musical implications as descriptive of harmonic phenomena apart from the myth that he was re-creating in music, and further he also considered his modes of limited transposition and his nonretrogradable rhythms to be pathways to a brilliant species of "theological rainbow": "Let us think now of the hearer of our modal and rhythmic music.... [I]n spite of himself he will submit to the strange charm of impossibilities: a certain effect of tonal ubiquity in the nontransposition, a certain unity of movement (where beginning and end are confused because identical) in the nonretrogradation, all things which lead him progressively to that sort of *theological rainbow* which the musical language, of which we seek edification and theory, attempts to be."[24]

The identification of Piroutcha with "mon souffle" ("my breath") in line 6 of "Doundou tchil" not only positions the beloved as the man's source of life and wholeness, but also it provides a connection with Wagner's *Tristan and Isolde*. To be sure, Messiaen's French verses cannot hope to achieve the polarity of breathing and world spirit in the German text of the last act of Wagner's music drama in which, dying, Isolde sings:

Wie sie [Düfte] schwellen,
mich umrauschen,
soll ich atmen,
soll ich lauschen?

34 Olivier Messiaen and the Tristan Myth

 . . .
In dem wogenden Schwall,
in dem tönenden Schall,
in des Welt Atems
wehendem All—,
ertrinken,
versinken—,
unbewusst—,
höchste Lust![25]

(As [the fragrances] swell and swirl around me, should I breathe
them, should I listen? . . . In the surging wave, in the resounding
vibration, in the World Spirit's depths encompassing All—drown-
ing, sinking, unknowingly—greatest joy!)

Such a sustained paean of desire is not present in Song 4 of *Harawi*, but
nevertheless, as in Wagner's music drama, at its heart is the notion attributed to the lovers that life for the one cannot be lived without the
other. Hence reference to the beloved in this song is by means of beneficent images. She is fruit, and she is the light ("lumière"), the latter image
reminiscent of the "star-linked" beloved of "Bonjour toi, colombe verte"
(Song 2). The symbolism extends to the passages played by the pianist
alone, without the voice, when the composer directs the performer to
play passages of shimmering chords "like glass" (*comme du verre*).

The song's final line of verse breaks away from the "doundou tchil"
of ankle bells of the previous line: "Toungou, mapa, nama, mapa, kahipipas." This is a combination of Quechua and Sanskrit words, mainly
chosen for their sound rather than their sense. "Toungou" is another
onomatopoetic word, signifying the soft roulades of the dove, according
to the d'Harcourts,[26] while "mapa" seems to be a synthetic word made
up by the composer out of two Sanskrit syllables, both standing for intervals in the Hindu musical scale. "Nama" too may be traced to two
syllables designating the Hindu scale but may also be a word in Sanskrit
meaning "name," and "kahipipas" in Quechua signifies "here," used in
the expression "here or there" ("kahipipas, mahipipas"). The Quechua
words are derived from the song "Tikata Tarpuinikiču."[27] In "Syllabes"
(Song 8), both words and musical intervals of this phrase are borrowed
and transformed, though in Song 4 there seem to be no musical echoes
(Example 2.3).

Example 2.3

TIKATA TARPUINIKIČU

Until the advent of minimalism and the popularity of such composers as John Tavener, Philip Glass, and Arvo Pärt, few aside from Ravel in his *Bolero* would perhaps risk, as Messiaen did, the danger of monotony by the many repetitions of "doundou tchil" on one note. He simply presented the song, with and without changes, its build-up of tempo and volume, and then left the listener to become hypnotically caught up in the regular beat of the dance. This song concludes the first unit of songs in which the texts, like an inverted verse rainbow, trace the *persona*'s descent from an experience of happiness into anxiety and despair and then to recovery. Song 4 also anticipates the next song, "L'amour de Piroutcha."

PART II

Song 5

The words and music of the entire group of Songs 5 through 9 are characterized by anxiety in spite of calm in the apparent lullaby in the Young Girl's segment of "L'amour de Piroutcha." Messiaen's text for "L'amour de Piroutcha" is presented in dialogue:

Young Girl: Toungou, ahi, toungou, rock-a-bye, you, my cinder of light,
Rock-a-bye your little one in your green arms.
Piroutcha, your little cinder, for you.

Young Man: Your eye all the heavens, doundou tchil.
Cut off my head, doundou tchil.
Our sighs, blue and gold, Ahi!
Chains of red, black, mauve, love, death.

The word 'toungou' is imitative of the cooing of the dove and is derived from the Quechua song "Tungu, Tungu."[28] The melody, however, utilizes borrowings from the pentatonic Quechua song "Piruča," built on four regularly used tones, D–F–A–C, and G, which is used less frequently[29] (Examples 2.4 and 2.5). Messiaen took over the five tones and used them as the basis for his vocal line in the section expressing the thoughts and feelings of the young girl. In his song, the soft cooing "Toungou, ahi" on a minor third as in a call seems at first to belie the inner turbulence that shortly will emerge when the young man, in the lines given to him in the dialogue says, "Coupe-moi la tête" ("Cut off my head"), and lists "Chaînes rouges, noires, mauves," red, black, and mauve—imagery that at first glance suggests "la mort" rather than "l'amour." It is a strange response to the girl's speech, which admittedly in itself is ambiguous and even at first confusing. One might wonder about the identity of "ma cindre des lumières" ("my cinder of light"). Who is the little one being rocked "in your green arms" ("berce la petite en tes bras verte") as in a lullaby? But then in her final line she seems to indicate that this is the girl herself—and she tells her name: "Piroutcha, your little cinder." The effect is of characters blurring in and out of one and the other, like the confusion of identities in Surrealist paintings and even more especially in Surrealist films. The flattened corpse turning

Example 2.4

Example 2.5

into a cardboard figure in Salvadore Dali and Luis Buñuel's *Un Chien Andalou* may be recalled.[30] But there is also another way of interpreting the cinder image that is surely more significant; as an equivalent of emotion, the "cinder of light" also may describe the glowing passion of the lovers.

The young man's words are, to be sure, in the spirit of Surrealism and not susceptible to purely rational explanation. For example, "ton œil tous les ciels" ("your eye all the heavens") reminds one of those Surrealist works of art in which an eye (or eyes) dominates the entire painting.[31] Goléa interprets the strange command "cut off my head" as representative of the desire to be rid of the instrument of thoughts and feelings, the head with the brain: "Cut off my head ... cut off the seat of all sensibility, of all mobility, of all sensuality, of all pleasure."[32] Messiaen has described the "sighs, blue and gold," as the "sighs of the two lovers which approach each other, which touch each other, which mingle their sighs, their sighs blue and gold, blue, the color of blood under the skin which swells at the call of love, gold, the color of the aroused flesh which warms, which flames, which burns, which ripens in the sun of love."[33] Messiaen also intended the "Chaînes rouges, noires, mauves"—the words are set to descending intervals of different sizes, including the tritone—to be identified with the mountains of the Dauphiné region where he spent his childhood,[34] but surely he also had in mind the Andes, which are the setting of the Peruvian folklore upon which he was drawing so heavily. In any case, the dialogue expresses love and death, and one is forced in the midst of the beauty of the mountains to face the fact that the culmination of life is in fact death. The symbolism is carried over into the melody, for on "la mort," which had leaped down a seventh from D to E, there is now a descent by means of an acciaccatura from E to the D immediately below it. One goes down into death. As the man's words are sung a second time, "la mort" only sinks as far as G, and the song ends on an added sixth chord in G major, giving the ending a very solid G major tonal feeling and setting up an impression of rest after all the wanderings through the composer's Modes of Limited Transpositions and chromaticisms.

Song 6

"Répétition planétaire" opens with an untranslatable forest cry— "Ahi"—and repetition of the Quechua and Sanskirt syllables "Mapa, nama, mapa, nama," followed by "lila" (a Quechua word, also reminiscent of Sanskrit 'lîla,' meaning play)[35] and ending with "tchil," which again evokes ankle bells.

> Ahi! O Mapa nama mapa nama lila, tchil.
> Straddle a black cry.
> Black echo of time,
> Cry before the earth at any moment,
> Black echo of time,
> Winding staircase.
> Whirlpool,
> Red star,
> Whirlpool,
> Planet consumes in turning.

In spite of the references to planets and dance, this song seems more closely linked with "Montagnes" (Song 3) in its insistence upon the image of blackness. Yet the mood here is more of inward and outward churning, emotional upheaval, and outer pressures, rather than the pure despair of "Montagnes," and the mood is modified by other images, the "Winding staircase" ("Escalier tournant") and the "Whirlpool" ("Tourbillon"). The staircase, which will return in the ninth song of the cycle ("L'escalier redit, gestes du soleil"), may be the staircase of time, of

Example 2.6

heaven, and of water, but here it seems primarily to represent the inward spiraling that the soul undergoes in order to achieve balance when all seems to reel around it. The turbulence (the "vertige" of "Montagnes") that the person is experiencing is cosmic. Goléa discovers in this poem the "prodigious shock of the cosmos, which is translated into music with an immense rhythmic power, a sonorous and unsurpassed frenzy," and which "is continued in a commentary that succeeds in reuniting in a sheaf the cries, the colors, the prodigious movement of the rhythm of love and death in both the universe and man."[36] More immediately connected to the structure of the cycle, however, is the "Echo noir du temps" ("the black echo of time"), which clearly is associated with imagery of the Abyss and with Messiaen's preoccupation with time. Anxiety, which is the emotion being dramatized here, cannot exist in eternity, but it is in fact a condition of living in time. To experience anxiety in time thus is to enter into the abyss of time; fortunately, this may take place in a manner which may ultimately insure a reintegration of the personality more aware than ever before of its consciousness.

Messiaen's musical setting must connect his words and their meaning once again to a musical texture that will express emotional upheaval in which even the planets reel and turn about the *persona*. The metaphors of the text must be expressed in appropriate musical metaphors—that is, in a structure including melody, harmony, and rhythm, which are expressive of cosmic love. The beginning thus integrates primitive cries and forest calls consisting of thirty-second notes in fourths (perfect and augmented fourths and a diminished fifth) which are built on descending thirds and seconds. Messiaen provides an effective musical equivalent for the repeated wild "appel en forêt," unforgettable—even blood curdling—in the best performances of this song, which begins with the repeated cry "Ahi!" followed by the syllable "O" (Example 2.6). The effect achieved by the calls seems very elemental, almost like a brutal yodel, albeit one based on less tonal intervals than the yodel. They are followed by the Quechua and Sanskrit syllables that function like an invented language—words set to accompanying music that, repeated over and

Example 2.7

ADIEU

over, is intended to be mysterious and incantatory. Thereafter, the section of the song that presents the lovers as reeling planets is disjunctive and strange. Ultimately the shape of the song is circular, out of which there is no musical release except in a complete halt by the accompaniment. Four cries, a forest call, and a last arpeggio in the lower register of the keyboard serve to complete the song.

Song 7

A goodbye, addressed to the green dove, is announced at the beginning of Song 7, entitled "Adieu," but it is of course not a final parting, as the remainder of the cycle demonstrates (Example 2.7). The text may be translated as follows:

> Goodbye to you, green dove;
> Sorrowful angel.
> Goodbye to you, limpid pearl,
> Guardian sun.
> You, of night, of fruit, of heaven, of day,

Wing of love.
Goodbye to you, new light,
Philter with two voices.
Star-linked,
Shadow-sharing,
In my hand my fruit of heaven, of day,
Faraway love.
Goodbye to you, my heaven on earth,
Goodbye to you, desert which weeps,
Mirror without sigh of love.
Of flower, of night, of fruit, of heaven, of day,
Forever.

The experience of parting, as when Tristan and Iseult must leave each other's presence in most retellings of the Tristan story, cannot be avoided. The anxiety attendant upon this parting will, however, look forward to the concluding songs of the cycle when in the tenth song the link to heaven becomes actualized and when in the eleventh song the stars jump joyously.

Familiar images return in "Adieu," as in such phrases as "perle limpide" ("limpid pearl"), "Toi, de nuit, de fruit, de ciel, de jour" ("you, of night, of fruit, of heaven, of day"), "Étoile enchaînée" ("Star-linked"), and "Ombre partagée" ("Shadow-sharing") from "Bonjour toi, colombe verte" (Song 2). The "miroir" of "Doundou tchil" (Song 4) returns as "miroir sans souffle d' amour" ("mirror without sigh of love"), but there are new images as well: the "Ange attristé" ("sorrowful angel"), "Soleil gardien" ("Guardian sun"), "Philtre à deux voix" ("Philter with two voices"), and "désert qui pleure" ("desert which weeps"). These images are inherently sad, but, in invoking the philter, the composer clearly has the love potion of the Tristan story in mind as the source of the mood. In Wagner's version of the story, the potion is imbibed in Act 1, where neither the hero nor the heroine understands its true nature. It is neither a death drink, as Isolde believes, nor a drink of friendship, as Tristan believes. Its use by Wagner was severely criticized by critics such as Eduard Hanslick, who objected to the canceling of the free will of the hero and heroine which was seen as inappropriate in a drama.[37] But for Messiaen the philter was embraced as a symbol that represented an event in the lives of the lovers that is beyond rational control and beyond logical explanation. Yet for him the philter was not causal in a magical sense. It was a symbol of the spontaneous erupting of a love that causes long periods of anxiety but also produces moments of bliss. As a commentator on Gottfried von Strassburg's version of the Tristan story has remarked, the love potion is "a metaphor for that psychological moment in love when two people of strongly sensual disposition lose control of the human faculty of free choice, under the influence of an already vehement, unsuspected, inward approach to each other, and the tides of passion that have been stored in the unconscious flood together, submerging them, who have lost all power of will. . . . This psychological process . . . is elevated by the poet into an objective experience of an existential absolute and described as an independent force, more than human, opening out to the transcendent."[38]

The love released when the philter is consumed is a kind of frenzy that is nevertheless heroic, but it also has a demonic side to it. It is the uncontrollable passion that, as they were reading of Lancelot's love for Queen Guinevere, had taken hold of Paolo and Francesca in Dante's *Inferno* (Canto 5: 124–38). Passion of this sort is potentially destructive. Yet for Messiaen it was also "star-linked," and the beloved in a sense is rightly called an "angel." It is the transcendent aspect of this anguished love that makes the apotheosis of the lovers possible later in the song cycle.

The tune that underlies the A section of "Adieu" is derived from "Delirio," which, as noted above, is also used in Songs 2 and 12. The setting of the images of the poem in "Adieu" is straightforward, with the line "Philtre à deux voix" being set to the melodic interval of a tritone, which, as noted, was not for Messiaen a sign of the demonic in spite of its ambiguity here. Nevertheless, the association of the philter with the tritone seems to be no accident, though this musical device is not tied to this object as a leitmotif. Following section A, there are two piano interludes, which may be identified as B and C. These interludes are genuinely different from the earlier rhapsodic bird song of "Bonjour toi, colombe verte" (Song 2). In the section marked *un peu vif* there is a deliberate feeling of a lack of purpose as the rhythm moves from triplet eighths to eighth notes to sixteenths. Here the chords and rhythms are directed to be played "like bells" (*comme des cloches*). The next section for piano alone (C), marked *très modéré*, has dissonant chords of superpositions crowned by a chord, preceded by acciaccaturas, to be played "like a tam-tam" (*"comme un Tam-Tam"*). Section B for the piano is repeated a total of seven times and section C four times, alternating with two inversions of A. The last A section flies high at "pleure" ("weeps") and descends at "d'amour" ("of love") and "de jour" ("of the day"). Two goodbyes in the text identify the beloved as "de ciel de terre" ("my heaven on earth") and, less conventionally, as a "désert qui pleure" ("desert which weeps"). The images of "flower," "night," "fruit," "heaven," and "day" are reprised, and the text ends with the words "pour toujours" ("forever").

As Messiaen approached the close of the song, he rejected the idea of bringing back old material in favor of introducing new, marked *"un peu plus lent."* The section is not like anything in Songs 2 or 12, or like anything else encountered in "Adieu" up to this point. The new section consists of only two dissonant chords, which rock back and forth in both rapid (shorter note values) and slow (longer note values) motion. These two chords may represent the philter "à deux voix." Thereafter Messiaen reiterates an A-like section and finally closes the piece with three acciaccatura-graced polytonal chords.

Song 8

"Syllabes" plays a unique function in the cycle since it embodies a warning analogous to Brangäne's "Habet acht" in Act 2 of *Tristan und Isolde,* but in this case is distanced and transformed through an example of the "friendly animal" motif of folklore. Specifically, the animal is a monkey—or, rather, monkeys in the plural—of Andean legend. In this folkloric example, the monkeys warn an Inca prince of danger and thus save his life.[39] To be sure, such helpful monkeys are quite unusual, for these creatures are more often than not seen as tricksters and as generally unhelpful to humans.[40] But the event is striking in other ways, including in the use of the word "pia" that is passed by the creatures from tree to tree to warn the prince. This again is an onomatopoetic word, repeated again and again, along with the Quechua words "kahipipas," "mahipipas," and "doundou tchil." Together these repetitions form the basis for a substantial part of the song, which had begun with the invocation once again to the green dove, also identified as the "violette double" ("double of the violet"), a flower to be treasured. And her name here is Piroutcha.

Green dove,
The number five to you,
The double of the violet will double,
Very far, very low.
O my heaven, you flower,
Piroutcha mia!

44   Olivier Messiaen and the Tristan Myth

Let us spread out from heaven,
Piroutcha mia!
Let us blossom from water,
Piroutcha mia!
Kahipipas, mahipipas,
Pia, pia, pia, doundou tchil [repeated].

But why is Piroutcha associated with the number five in the line "La chiffre cinq à toi" ("The number five to you")? The number symbolism seems quite deliberate. "Is it an astral symbol?" asks Goléa.[41]

Messiaen's number symbolism, however, is not usually so arcane. Tanneguy de Quénetain calls attention especially to the symbolism inherent in the order of the pieces in *Vingt regards sur l'enfant Jesus*: "the sixth piece, which evokes creation by the Word ('without which nothing was made') is in this particular position because the numerical six is the number for the Creation."[42] The fifth piece in *Vingt regards* is labeled "Regard du Fils sur le Fils," and is accompanied by the following explanation: "Mystery, ray of light in the night— . . . the person of the Word in human nature—marriage of the human and divine natures in Jesus Christ. The *Theme of God* underlies two sets of homophonic chords which form a rhythmic canon by the addition of dots to the second set of chords."[43] Thus in this instance the (uneven) number five was associated for Messiaen with duality, especially as expressed in the two natures of Christ. In his earlier *Poèmes pour Mi* and *Chants de Terre et de Ciel*, the same principle of duality had been translated into a struggle between spiritual and physical, a struggle characterized by very human anguish. In Song 8 of *Harawi*, in which the number five is attributed to the beloved, she is hence also visualized in terms of a duality that is divided between heaven and earth, struggling with spiritual and physical realities. A further level of meaning may also be related to Messiaen's deep sensitivity to Catholic theology and symbolism, since in medieval iconography the number five commonly referred to the five wounds of Christ.[44] The association of the number five with the Passion means that it may well have been connected in the composer's mind with pain, suffering, and anguish, and at the same time he may have seen the number as indicating experience leading to a goal that is ultimately desirable.

The desirability of the beloved is expressed through the metaphor of a flower, a double violet, which will double. In the expansive mood of love, everything the beloved touches blossoms ("O mon ciel tu fleuris"), and the lovers themselves wish to spread out from heaven ("O déplions du ciel") like a beautiful rainbow. The reference to water ("O fleurissons de l'eau") connects this song with "Bonjour toi, colombe verte," where water is linked to fertile images of fruit and flower and to the spiritual image of heaven. Furthermore, this song is also related to "L'escalier redit, gestes du soleil" (Song 9), where connections between water, time, and heaven are created by the composer through constant reiteration and juxtaposition and through the deliberate use of parallel phrases such as "L'œil de l'eau" ("Eye of water"), "L'œil du temps" ("Eye of time"), and "L'œil du ciel" ("Eye of heaven"). Following the first complete statement of the text comes the warning word of the monkeys. There are 275 repetitions of their word "pia," all on a single tone; toward the end of the warning, the tempo accelerates and the dynamics increase. The directions to the singer and accompanist are *pressez beaucoup* and *crescendo molto*. The effect is one of climax through accumulation, acceleration, and increase of volume. I do not believe that a single word had ever been used previously in Western vocal music to create just this effect and to build such a musical structure. One may think of certain repetitions in dance music and the purely instrumental repetitions in Ravel's *Bolero*, which repeats a melodic phrase tirelessly with an ostinato rhythm that is only broken at the very end by the addition of a striking modulation. The warning in *Harawi*, however, also is reminiscent of the Balinese monkey chant, the *Kečak*, which not only is built on a single syllable ("čak," however, and not "pia"), but is also sung hocket style by the monkeys and with similar repetition.[45]

In its function of warning the lovers, however, the monkey chant is also directly analogous to Brangäne's warning in Wagner's music drama—a warning that is ultimately related to the traditional dawn song or *alba*, sung by the lovers' friend or confidant to signify the coming of the dawn or the danger to them—not infrequently danger from the arrival on the scene of the lady's husband. Such a song, for example, is the troubadour Guiraut de Bornehl's "Reis glorios." According to Jonathan Saville, such an *alba* represents the call of Conscience to lovers who are entirely immersed in pleasure and who are faced with separation:

This separation takes place in time, and is due to time. The sun, rising, *is* time; and because of it the lovers must part. If the lovers had their way, if the pleasure principle ruled the universe, nothing would ever change, no one would ever grow old, the love affair—and, indeed, this single night of the love affair—would go on forever. The lovers want to reject time, to blot it out. But the movement of time appears at the very foundation of the dramatic events in the *alba*: the change from night to day, the dawn itself. . . . The night of union changes to the day of separation; there is no stasis in human life; the joy of love cannot last; and, finally, life itself must give way—in the process of time—to death. The lovers do not want to accept time; but the watchman, proponent of the reality principle, keeps reminding them of the existence of time, keeps telling them that in the world of nature time cannot be avoided.[46]

Messiaen would surely have rejected some of the preconceptions involved in Saville's analysis but otherwise might well have found his description of the *alba* to be a useful though partial commentary on the duality that is present in "Syllabes." The composer's reservations would center on the depiction of love as entirely *pleasure*, for he consistently insisted on the connection between earthly love and the spiritual element.[47]

Song 9

The ninth song in the cycle, "L'escalier redit, gestes du soleil," brings closure to the second unit of songs that had begun with "L'amour de Piroutcha" (Song 5). It is particularly significant because here Messiaen deals most directly with the love-death material he had found in the Tristan story, especially as it had appeared in Wagner's music drama. The importance of the song is also underscored by its placement as the ninth in the sequence of twelve, since for the composer the number nine held a special significance as indicative of both maternity and time. Thus the ninth piece in his *Vingt regards sur l'enfant Jesus* is entitled "Regard du Temps" and is described as follows: "The mystery of the fullness of time: Time which sees the birth of the One who is eternal. There are two musical ideas which are developed in turn: a theme with different phrase lengths, and a rhythmic canon."[48] As the number for the incarnation of Christ, therefore, the number nine particularly links together ideas of transcendence and time in a manner that stresses the human predicament—the condition of creatures living in time with its distorting power and its ability to cause anguish in the soul. A translation of Song 9 follows:

1. It no longer speaks, the staircase smiles,
Each step toward the south.

Harawi: Song of Love and Death 47

Of heaven, of water, of time, staircase of time.
Its eye is wasteland, light in secret.
Clear stone and clear sun.
Of water, of time, of heaven,
    staircase of heaven.
You, my little cinder, are there,
    your temples green, mauve, on the water.
Like death.
Eye of water.

2. The staircase repeats, gestures of the sun,
Color of new silence.
Of water, of time, of heaven,
    staircase of heaven.
I wait in greenness,
    starred by love.
It is so simple being dead.
Of time, of heaven, of water,
    staircase of water.
My little cinder, you are there,
    your temples green, mauve, on time.
Like death.
Eye of time.

Of heaven, of water, of time,
Your present eye which breathes,
Of water, of time, of heaven,
The heart of the clock goes mad.
Death is there, my green dove.
Death is there, my limpid pearl.
Death is there.
We sleep far from time in your gaze.
I am dead.

3. Water will pass over our heads,
    guardian sun.
Fire eats our sighs.
Philter of two voices.
Our glances from beginning to end,
    seen by death.
Let us invent the love of the world.

So we may seek ourselves,
So we may mourn ourselves,
So we may dream ourselves,
So we may find ourselves.
Of heaven, of water, of time,
Your heart which beats,
   my fruit, my portion of darkness,
   you are here, you.
Love, joy!

4. Silence is dead,
   embrace the time.
Sun of joyless cries.
Of time, of heaven, of water,
Gaiety flourishes in the arms of heaven.
Fan in the guise of a birdsong.
Of heaven, of water, of time,
Staircase of time.
My little cinder, you are here.
   your temples green, mauve, on heaven,
   on heaven, on heaven,
   your temples on heaven,
Like death.
Eye of heaven.

The lovers in this song, which is the longest of the cycle, descend—
"Chaque marche vers le sud" ("Each step toward the south")—the Staircase of Time. Time *is* the staircase along which they fall *into* love and
move downward toward their love-death, and as they do so they are
described as being "Du temps, du l'eau, du ciel" ("Of water, of time, of
heaven"). As Robert Sherlaw Johnson observes, "The ritual aspects" of
this song (as in "Doundou tchil") "become intensely more ecstatic . . .
embracing the sky, the water, and the whole of time in the recurrent
refrain. . . . Love unites the lovers to each other and to the love of the
whole world: 'Inventons l'amour du monde' ('let us find the love of the
world')."[49] Although the precise nature of the love-death in this song is
not specified, it may have one or more interpretations. The ambiguity of
the text may be deliberate. Messiaen may have implied any one of the
following choices: (1) It is a real death of the lovers, as suggested by such
lines as "I am dead." (2) It is the fear of death that is involved—the fear

with which we must come to terms in the process of "seek[ing] our-selves." (3) It is a metaphorical death such as is encountered in sexual ecstasy, a death that has been understood phenomenologically in terms of a return to chaos and reintegration. In any case, this poem, which represents the highest point of anxiety in the cycle, keeps death before us as a constant presence. Repeated like a litany are the words "La mort est là": "La mort est là, ma colombe verte./ La mort est là, ma perle limpide. / La mort est là" ("Death is there, my green dove. Death is there, my limpid pearl. Death is there").

"C'est si simple d'être mort" ("It is so simple being dead"), says the *persona* in the second stanza. In stanza 3 his death wish seems to have been realized when he says, "Je suis mort" ("I am dead"). The lovers' amorous glances have been seen by death, and hence has come about this union of love and death. Nevertheless, in spite of the emphasis on mortality in this song, in spite of the anxieties of living that cry out for release, the text also expresses an affirmation of life. "L'amour, la joie!" ("Love, joy!"), exults the poet. The sun is "of joyous cries" ("Le soleil cris joyeux") and "Gaiety flourishes in the arms of heaven" ("La gaieté fleurit dans les bras du ciel"). If the composer intended us to understand a real death here, the death of the lovers nevertheless is an ascent into the omniscient "Eye of heaven" ("L'œil du ciel"), itself a symbol of a state of transcendence that is distinct from the temporal order. If the "stair-case," winding or circular, ascending or descending, is a symbol for time and the agony of life, then life itself is paradoxically also joyful. Existence is ecstasy.

The musical setting of "L'escalier redit, gestes du soleil" cannot, of course, free itself from time, from duration, which in Messiaen's view was to be regarded as the essence of music. The presence of time is affirmed even in the poetic structure of the text, consisting of four stanzas with regularly recurring repetitions and a longer refrain following stanza 2 that breaks the pattern of regularity set up in stanzas 1, 2, and 4, which are parallel in construction. The refrain, with its listing of water, heaven, and time, is set to the descending diminished fifth (e–A♯), an interval with varied and ambiguous meanings, one of them being traditionally the previously noted *diabolus in musica*. In one of the refrains the dimin-ished fifth will change from diminished fifth to a variety of rising and falling intervals.

Naturally, tempo, duration, and rhythmic values also assert the pres-ence of time. Since this is a song that, among other emotions, expresses joy, the beginning tempo is *Vif, joyeux et passionné*; contrasting with the

50   Olivier Messiaen and the Tristan Myth

fast tempo, the notes setting the first words, "Il ne parle plus" ("It no
longer speaks"), are very static: repeated b-flats with one "escape" note
to the step above and then returning to b♭. The static melody is coupled
with steady eighth-note values, with the escape note on the penultimate
eighth note of the phrase being lengthened by half its value (♪.). Messiaen has observed that the longer added values have the effect of re-
tarding the musical phrase,[50] and the effect here is the destruction of the
march-like rhythm set up by the eighth notes. At the words "Je suis
mort" ("I am dead"), the tempo slows (*poco ritenuto*), as it does again at
"Inventons l'amour du monde" ("Let's invent the love of the world"),
again marked *poco riten.* At the latter phrase, the melody soars high and
lingers long on the highest note at "monde." The huge agogic accent on
"monde" befits the ecstatic idea of inventing a "love of the world,"[51] a
love never before experienced, as the lovers believe it to be. Other means
of speeding or slowing the tempo are also found in this song; for example, at the words "mon fruit, ma part de ténèbres,/ tu es là" ("my
fruit, my portion of darkness, you are here") at the close of stanza 3, the
tempo is slowed by augmentation—one measure each of dotted eighth
notes, quarter notes, and dotted quarter notes.

Messiaen, in his use of his harmonic language, has set out to express
fully the tension and joyous release of his text. The chordal progressions
beneath the melodic line are quite dissonant, consisting of chords of superpositions, played by hands alternating to give a kind of leaping effect.
The dissonant chords, ending with a chord that can be spelled enhar-
monically in both E and E♭, sound as if they are within the context of
the key of E♭ major. Messiaen's musical setting thus itself provides an
apt metaphor for experience and emotion in a work that is extremely
conscious of time—and, more specifically, aware of the pain of time and
the need to endure through pain and anxiety to resolution and joy.

In the final stanza, material is repeated with some development by
elimination from the first stanza at the words "Le silence est mort." Then
the song closes with twenty-three repetitions of a triplet ostinato theme
over a long-held and later repeated pedal, a tonic chord in the second
inversion with an added sixth. The words "Comme la mort. / L'œil du
ciel" ("Like death. Eye of heaven") are set to the same notes and rhythmic values as in their earlier appearance, but they are given importance
and finality in the way the line resolves upward instead of downward.

Harawi: Song of Love and Death　　　51

PART III

Song 10

"Amour oiseau d'étoile" initiates the final group of songs in *Harawi*, which will celebrate the apotheosis of the lovers. Agony and guilt have not been entirely purged away, but the imagery now is of heaven, bird, star—all images of transcendence.

> Bird of the star,
> Your eye which sings,
> Toward the stars,
> Your head reversed under heaven.
> Your eye of star,
> Links falling,
> Toward the stars,
> Shortest pathway from shadow to heaven.
> All the birds of the stars,
> Far from the painting, my hands sing,
> Star, silence augments from heaven,
> My hands, your eye, your neck, heaven.

The principal inspiration for the text of this song has been identified as a Surrealist painting usually entitled *The Invisible Isle*, painted in 1936 by Roland Penrose (Figure 1).[52] Messiaen had seen a reproduction of the painting in a Swiss periodical, *Forme et Coleur*, and was struck with it. The painting shows, in the foreground, a disembodied head of a young woman hanging downward[53] from the dark sky with a new moon, stars, and white clouds at the top of the canvas. In the center is a tiny island with small buildings, and the long hair of the disproportionately larger head hangs down onto the island and envelops it. From the bottom of the painting, a man's hands reach up toward the hair. Typically, Messiaen chose to interpret the latent symbolism in the painting as an attempt to bring together the heavenly and the earthly, the spiritual and the physical. All of the phrases and images of Song 10 are related in some way to the painting. "Ta tête à l'envers sous le ciel" ("Your head reversed under heaven") identifies the woman's head with the beloved of the song cycle. Other images, such as the birds and stars, are not only links between heaven and earth but also serve as agents of rescue that are able to assist one out of the abyss. In this instance, the beloved is addressed as "Oiseau d'étoile" ("Bird of the star"), and her eye "sings / Toward the stars" ("Ton œil qui chante / Vers les étoiles").

The importance of eyes in *Harawi* cannot be overestimated. Since the Middle Ages, lovers have often been presented gazing into each other's eyes. In his *Vita nuova*, Dante had spoken of "the most noble power" of Beatrice's eyes as encompassing Love and its origin.[54] Gottfried von Strassburg's Tristan and Isolde thus exchange amorous glances: "When from time to time they tried to observe each other through eyes which Love had limed, their flesh assumed the hue of their hearts and souls." Further: "One look, one tender glance from the eyes of one's beloved will surely quench a myriad pangs of body and of soul. One kiss from one's darling's lips that comes stealing from the depths of her heart— how it banishes love's cares!"[55] In "La ville qui dormait, toi" (Song 1) Messiaen had written the words "L'œil immobile, sans denouer ton regard" ("The eye immobile, without unraveling your glance"), while "Ton œil tous les ciels" ("Your eye all the heavens") had appeared in "L'amour de Piroutcha" (Song 5). The eye also had been a means of communication between husband and wife—the language of the eyes, which is as important as shared thoughts—in *Poèmes pour Mi*, in which the *persona* had said, "Et un œil près de mon œil, / une pensée près de ma pensée" ("And an eye close to my eye, a thought close to my thought"). Eyes are likewise a metaphor for the physical bond that unites a couple in the song "Bail avec Mi," dedicated to his first wife, in *Chants de Terre et de Ciel*: "Ton œil de terre, / mon œil de terre" ("Your mortal eye, my mortal eye"). In Song 10 of *Harawi*, however, the eye as a symbol of lovers' glances is juxtaposed with symbols of transcendence. In the Penrose painting, the eye is near heaven—hence it is like both bird and star— and because it is like a bird, presumably it is able to sing. The opening lines of Messiaen's song assert: "Oiseau d'étoile, / Ton œil qui chante . . ." ("Bird of the star, / Your eye which sings . . .").

"Loin du tableau mes mains chantent" ("Far from the painting my hands sing"), Messiaen wrote, referring to the painting by Penrose but also perhaps implying the hands of a musician. In the last line of the song, the man's hands, the woman's eye, her neck, and heaven are all connected; as in the painting, the hands nearly touch the woman's hair, with her neck disappearing into clouds and forming a link with heaven. The painting thus provided the visual stimulus for an important aspect of the song that begins the final section of *Harawi*, for here the lovers rise above their anxiety. There is nothing here of the final act of Wagner's music drama, for Messiaen had an alternate conclusion in mind for his lovers.

The use by a composer of a painting or visual depiction as inspiration for music was not, of course, something new. A number of Debussy's works were directly derived from visual images, one of the most memorable being the three *Nocturnes* of 1897–1900 (*Nuages, Fêtes,* and *Sirènes*) inspired by clouds, a festival, and Homer's sirens singing on the rocks. Debussy's painting of pictures in sound is always very subtle, but Messiaen in "Amour oiseau d'étoile" is equally subtle in connecting the visual to musical sounds, especially in the musical metaphors that link earth to heaven. Of these there are two, one structural and the other harmonic. Bird songs are used to provide musical associations for the many references to birds, stars, and heaven, and he used the *Bar* form, AAB, as in the *Minnelied* and in later German song. The two A sections consist of four phrases, each followed by a passage of bird song in thirty-second, sixteenth, eighth, and triplet sixteenth notes, while the voice below holds a long note. Then the A section is repeated, almost verbatim. The B section, consisting of four new phrases, has different passages of bird song following each phrase. Tempo also plays a role here, for the beginning of the song is marked *"Presque lent, avec charme et tendresse, trés pure"* ("Rather slow, with charm and tenderness, and very pure"). The harmonic metaphors involve chords of the dissonant, enchaining type used so frequently throughout the cycle. The chords here become harmonic litanies in the sense of providing different chords for each of the repeated tones of the voice; these consist of a dominant seventh chord in the second inversion, followed by, in the left hand, a dissonant cluster chord (including adjacent major and minor seconds) against, in the right hand, a chord with the implications of a raised supertonic in the second inversion. The third chord is a whole tone chord, with its lowest note on A♮. All of these rest on an F♯ tonic chord with added sixth.

The rhythmic technique used in the A sections of this song involves gradually augmenting the rhythm steadily from note to note throughout a phrase, beginning with an eighth note, proceeding to a quarter note, a dotted quarter note, a half note, and ending with a half note tied to an eighth note. This device is used in six of the twelve phrases in sections A and A^1. The B section is less mechanical rhythmically than the A sections. Each phrase is longer than the last, and in addition the practice of augmenting each note is dropped. The rhythm of each phrase differs slightly from every other, but most begin with an eighth note, followed

Example 2.8

Theme 1

Ka - tchi - ka - tchi les é - toi - les,

by one or more quarter notes; then, a dotted quarter, falling near the cadence, tends to delay the resolution. All of these synthesized but seemingly free phrases are juxtaposed with the total rhythmic freedom of the bird song passages, and the effect of the combination is of tranquility and transcendence.

Song 11

"Katchikatchi les étoiles" provides a strong contrast in mood and musical materials to the previous song. Here again Messiaen chose to borrow heavily from Peruvian sources to set the leaping image at "Katchikatchi" with nonretrogradable rhythms—irrational and uneven in value (Example 2.8).

> Katchikatchi the stars,
>   make them jump,
> Katchikatchi the stars,
>   make them dance.
> Katchikatchi the atoms,
>   make them jump,
> Katchikatchi the atoms,
>   make them dance.
> Nebulae spiral,
>   hands of my hair.
> Electrons, ants, arrows,
>   the silence in two.
> Alpha of the Centaur,
>   Betelgeuse, Aldebaran,
> Expand the space, rainbow
>   blusterer of time,
> Ionized laughter fury of the clock

Example 2.9

to the absent murder.
Cut off my head,
    its number rolls in blood!
Tou, ahi, mané, mani.

The word "katchikatchi" is Messiaen's adaptation of the Quechua "kačikačiča," in that context meaning grasshopper, as found in the second phrase of the dance-song "Mariposača Niñača"[56] (Example 2.9). However, for Messiaen the Quechua noun is used unsyntactically, as if it were changed into a verb for the purpose of linkage with the stars: "Katchikatchi les étoiles, / faites les sauter, / Katchikatchi les étoiles, / faites les danser" ("Katchikatchi the stars, / Make them jump, / Katchikatchi the stars, / Make them dance"). The description is of a cosmic dance where stars, planets, constellations, nebulae, atoms, and electrons leap about the sky in ecstatic movements. Dancing can be a source of power, an expression of a "compelling force," as Gerardus van der Leeuw has observed.[57] In the old cosmology the stars were believed to dance in the sky, and earthly dancing came to be understood as an imitation of the heavenly or cosmic dance in which "the celestial motion itself has been regarded as a dance."[58] Hence in Song 11 of *Harawi*, the lovers from the Tristan myth join in a heavenly dance, a cosmic *lîla*, which reflects the archetypal pattern. This transcendent dance is love, and it is power. The dance indeed becomes all-powerful, dominating the final songs in the cycle. Through the alchemy of metaphor, the earthly lovers have become stars and heavenly lovers. The music here involves a very high tessitura for the right hand accompaniment and a very low for the left, the wide separation suggesting the great height of the stars in comparison to the location of ordinary mortals on earth. The rhythm is jagged, symbolizing the leaping of the stars, and this effect is combined with the composer's nonretrogradable and added rhythms. Pairs of acciaccaturas precede some of the chords, again indicating the composer's intent to provide a musical equivalent for the leaping stars. Since the lovers are no longer mortal man and woman, "all is permitted to them," including the abandon of dancing and leaping.[59]

The verses of the song become more complex and more difficult to explicate after line 10 of the text, however. "Mains de mes cheveux" ("Hands of my hair") seems violently juxtaposed with the stars, atoms, nebulae, and electrons but is a bridge back to the Penrose painting, with the hands reaching up toward the hair. "Ants" ("fourmis") and "arrows" ("flèches") also appear to be strange partners, though the "flèches" are readily explained as the translation into French of the constellation Sagittarius, the star sign under which Messiaen was born.[60] No explanation is possible, however, for the ants except that they may be present as a surrealistic opposite or reconciliation of impossibles. Or, as in the case of the ants crawling out of the hand in Dali and Buñuel's surrealistic film *Un Chien Andalou*,[61] there may be no logical justification except as an expression of horror. Was Messiaen engaging in free association here? Nevertheless, the ants serve, like the repetition of "Cut off my head," as an indicator of underlying anxiety even here in the apotheosis of the lovers.

But there is even tension in the presentation of the stars that are singled out for attention, for these are "Alpha of the Centaur," Betelgeuse, and Aldebaran, three of the twenty-two brightest stars in the heavens. Here the chords are thicker, more dissonant, and leap even more wildly, as befitting these stars of the first magnitude. Betelgeuse, found near one shoulder of Orion, and Aldebaran, the right eye of Taurus, are red stars. Orion and Taurus are pictured in the older star maps as adversaries, with Orion brandishing a club and waving a scarf at the bull Taurus.[62] "Alpha of the Centaur," half a double star (the other half being called "Beta") appears in the constellation located in the southern sky between the Southern Cross and Hydra. The inclusion of this star suggests that it somehow resonated with Messiaen's interests, perhaps by citing the classical centaurs, whose physical characteristics joined the human and the animal.

In any case, the glory of the heavens and the joyful mood of cosmic dance stand in direct contrast to the next section with its return to the "Rire ionisé fureur d'horloge" ("Ionized laughter fury of the clock"). Once again the juxtaposition of the clock, a symbol of linear time, which in the modern world is understood as a kind of mad tyrant, with the death wish of "Coupez ma tête" comes as a shock. Goléa calls it a "terrible invocation."[63] When the head is cut off, its "number" (of which we are never apprised) "rolls in the blood" ("son chiffre roule dans le sang").

Harawi: Song of Love and Death   57

The regression to a less integrated state seems odd, though Messiaen may be merely entertaining a very "modern" impulse to avoid an idyllic ending by turning away once again from the kind of powerful resolution achieved in the earlier part of the song. The interjection of another excursion into Messiaen's synthetic language—"Tou, ahi! mané, mani"—perhaps is intended to introduce further fragmentation and dismemberment, in this instance separating "Tou" out of "Toungou," the Quechua word for the roulades of the dove. "Ahi" is the recurring cry from "L'amour de Piroutcha" and "Répétition planétaire" (Songs 5 and 6), here accompanied by a glissando, while about "Mané" we can only speculate, though we might suspect that it is the first word (meaning "God hath numbered thy kingdom, and finished it") in the French translation of the words written on the wall for King Nebuchadnezzar in Daniel 5: 25–26. If so, "mané" may be a prophecy of doom, perhaps related to the words that speak of the head, whose number "rolls in blood." But "mani," the final word in the song, is also the second word in the famous Tibetan mantra "Om mani padme hum," where it means "locked in the locust."[64] However, Messiaen may as well have used the word for its sound alone. The end of the song thus falls back into words that are truncated, signs of the nightmare with its transcendence-denying, insane clock against which Messiaen built up the structure of his song cycle. The conclusion thus is befitting the energy and anxiety generated by the words and music, which lead up to the singing of "Ahi" on c''', the highest note of the cycle.

Song 12

Although Messiaen said in his *Technique of My Musical Language* that he believed the sonata form to be obsolete, yet in the final song of *Harawi*, "Dans le noir," we find him making reference to the main points of the entire cycle not only in the text, which follows in translation, but also in the music.

In the dark, green dove,
In the dark, limpid pearl.
In the dark, my fruit of heaven, of day.
Distance of love.
My love, my breath!
Dove, green dove,
The number five is yours,

The double violet, doubled,
Very far, very deep.
The town which slept.

The music from the Peruvian song "Delirio"—familiar by this time in connection with the image of the green dove and because of its use in "Bonjour toi, colombe verte," "Adieu," and "L'escalier redit, gestes du soleil" (Songs 2, 7, and 9)—now sets the phrase "Dans le noir, colombe verte" ("In the dark, green dove"). Indeed, nothing new is presented in the text until the words "Mon amour, mon souffle" ("My love, my breath"), but even here there is an echo of "Doundou tchil" and "L'amour de Piroutcha" (Songs 4 and 5), while the melody too is reminiscent of the descending lines found, for example, in Songs 7 and 9; furthermore, the descending minor thirds are reminiscent of the melody for Song 5 at the words "Toungou, ahi, toungou." Further echoes are found from material throughout the cycle, including the use of the Quechua song "Tikata Tarpuinikiču." The only truly new musical material for the final song occurs in the accompaniment and in the interludes—each basically similar, with a constant rhythmic pattern of longer values in the right hand, and each succeeding interlude longer than the last—when the piano is heard without the voice. Thus the twelfth song may be demonstrated to be a grand recapitulation of musical and textual elements taken from the entire cycle.

Harawi is a remarkable *tour de force* lasting over fifty minutes and stretching the physical endurance and mental agility of both singer and accompanist to the utmost.[65] The twelve songs are a record of the composer's own struggles not only with the musical material but also with the problems of love and death (as announced in the subtitle that identifies the cycle as a *Chant d'amour et de mort*), which for him appeared to hold the key to the meaning of both life and art. The work seems out of step with the formalistic modernism of the middle of the twentieth century and is in many ways a precursor of certain of the concerns of present-day minimalists, particularly those who, like Tavener, Pärt, and Górecki, have returned to transcendental themes in their music. The similarities here involve the rejection of a formalism regarded as sterile and the development of musical equivalents for the composer's most deeply felt concerns. His own musical language was unique and was perfectly suited to exploring such matters as time and duration, which he understood in qualitative and psychological ways that were directly opposed

Harawi: Song of Love and Death 59

to the quantitive, chronometric, and scientific. And the translation of images itself became for him an exercise that could be effected by means of his modes of limited transposition, which reflect the boundedness of life as well as the necessity for escape and transcendence.

When *Harawi* is considered in the light of Messiaen's earlier work such as his *Quatuor pour la fin du temps*, its stylistic elements seem familiar in the presence of angels (for example, the angel who announces the end of time in the quartet), birds, and enchaining chords that are not chord progressions in the ordinary sense since they move from chord to chord without truly progressing—a way of indicating a circular link with infinity. But new to the song cycle is the unification of physical and spiritual joy—in spite of the anxiety and fear that are also evoked—which is not present in the composer's previous work. This material became available to Messiaen through his choice of the Tristan story as an armature around which he might enwrap his text and musical material. Furthermore, the Tristan material led him to Peruvian analogues, which he encountered through his discovery of the book by Raoul and Marguerite d'Harcourt. The Quechua songs are wondrously changed by the transforming prism of his art, and the transformation also opened the way for him to continue with the creation of two further compositions, *Turangalîla-symphonie* and *Cinq rechants*, which were to form the second and third parts of his Tristan trilogy.

NOTES

1. Olivier Messiaen, *Harawi* (Paris: Alphonse Leduc, 1948). Musical examples and quotations from the French text in the present chapter are by permission of the publisher, Alphonse Leduc.

2. Antoine Goléa, *Rencontres avec Olivier Messiaen* (Paris: Julliard, 1960), 123, 125; see also Pierrette Mari, *Olivier Messiaen* (Paris: Seghers, 1965), 117, 121. Along with Marcelle Bunlet, distinguished performers of *Harawi* have been Noelle Barker and Jane Manning. A recent recording has also been made by Lucy Shelton.

3. Messiaen chose the feminine voice to represent the states of man's soul (Goléa, *Rencontres*, 124). The choice is logical because the soul (*anima*) is traditionally regarded as feminine.

4. For further analysis of the music of *Harawi* as well as *Turangalîla-symphonie* and *Cinq rechants*, see Audrey Ekdahl Davidson, "Olivier Messiaen's Tristan Trilogy: Time and Transcendence," Ph.D. diss. (University of Minnesota, 1975).

5. The translations of the texts as presented here cannot always, of course, adequately express Messiaen's verse, which depends so much on the sound of the words that some have proclaimed *Harawi* to be untranslatable. I am grateful to David Collins for his assistance with my translations.

60   Olivier Messiaen and the Tristan Myth

6. Olivier Messiaen, *Music and Color: Conversations with Claude Samuel*, trans. E. Thomas Glasgow (Portland, Oregon: Amadeus Press, 1994), 110; see also Paul Griffiths, *Olivier Messiaen and the Music of Time*, (Ithaca: Cornell University Press, 1985), 23, and Anthony Pople, "Messiaen's Musical Language: An Introduction," in *The Messiaen Companion*, ed. Peter Hill (London: Faber and Faber, 1994), 18. A score of *Pelléas et Mélisande* was given to the young Messiaen by his teacher, Jehan de Gibon.

7. Claude Samuel, *Entretiens avec Olivier Messiaen* (Paris: Belfond, 1967), 43. For general comments and analysis of Messiaen's color symbolism, see Jonathan W. Bernard, "Messiaen's Synaesthesia: The Correspondence between Color and Sound in his Music," *Music Perception* 4 (1986): 41–68.

8. See Olivier Messiaen, *The Technique of My Musical Language*, trans. John Satterfield, 2 vols. (Paris: Alphonse Leduc, 1956), 1:37. See also ibid., 1:35, for development by elimination.

9. Wilfrid Mellers, *Caliban Reborn* (London: Gollancz, 1968), 35, 104.

10. Ibid., 35.

11. Raoul d'Harcourt and Marguerite d'Harcourt, *La Musique des Incas et ses survivances*, 2 vols. (Paris: Paul Geuthner, 1925), 1:190.

12. See Griffiths for the observation that "Delirio" "is very obviously the origin for the cycle's theme song . . ." (*Olivier Messiaen and the Music of Time*, 126–27).

13. D'Harcourt and d'Harcourt, *La Musique des Incas*, 1:189–90.

14. In the medieval *Roman de la Rose*, Venus's chariot was drawn by a team of doves; for other significances, see Louis Réau, *Iconographie de l'art Chrétien*, 3 vols. (Paris: Presses Universitaires de France, 1956), 1:102, and George Ferguson, *Signs and Symbols in Christian Art* (1954; reprint: Oxford University Press, 1961), 15–16.

15. Mircea Eliade, *Shamanism: Archaic Techniques of Ecstasy*, trans. Willard R. Trask, Bollingen Series 76 (Princeton: Princeton University Press, 1972), 89.

16. Samuel, *Entretiens*, 140.

17. Olivier Messiaen, Preface, *Quatuor pour la fin du temps* (Paris: Durand, 1942), i.

18. Bernard Gavoty and Olivier Messiaen, "Who Are You, Olivier Messiaen?" *Tempo* 58 (Summer 1961): 35.

19. D'Harcourt and d'Harcourt, *La Musique des Incas*, 2:458–59.

20. Messiaen, program notes for *Turangalîla-Symphonie* (Deutsche Grammophon compact disk 431 781–2), 5.

21. See Reidar Th. Christiansen, "Myth, Metaphor, and Simile," in *Myth: A Symposium*, ed. Thomas A. Sebeok (Philadelphia: American Folklore Society, 1955), 42–45.

22. Ferguson, *Signs and Symbols in Christian Art*, 43.

23. Messiaen, *The Technique of My Musical Language*, 1:52; see also Messiaen's Preface to *Quatuor pour la fin du temps*.

24. Messiaen, *The Technique of My Musical Language*, 1:21 (italics added).

25. For the music accompanying this text, see Richard Wagner, *Tristan und Isolde*, ed. Isolde Vetter, Sämtliche Werke 8, pts. 1–3 (Mainz: B. Schott's Söhne, 1990), 3: 172–77.

26. D'Harcourt and d'Harcourt, *La Musique des Incas*, 1:294.

27. Ibid., 2:493–94.

28. Ibid., 1:292–93.

29. Ibid., 1:276–77.

30. See the description of this scene in Luis Buñuel, *L'Age d'Or and Un Chien Andalou*, trans. Marianne Alexandre (New York: Simon and Schuster, 1968), 106–107, but the film must be consulted to observe this detail. See also Werner Spies, *Max Ernst–Loplop:The Artist's Other Self*, trans. Georges Braziller (London: Thames and Hudson, 1983).

31. See, for example, Max Ernst's drawing *The Wheel of Light* (Werner Spies and Helmut Rudolf Leppien, *Max Ernst Oeuvre-Katalog*), 3 vols. (Cologne: DuMont Schauberg, 1975), no. 818; and also William S. Rubin, *Dada, Surrealism, and Their Heritage* (New York: Museum of Modern Art, 1968), 91, fig. 88.

32. Goléa, *Rencontres*, 161.

33. Ibid.

34. Ibid.

35. For discussion of the term *lîla* (as play, but in a cosmic sense, and also love), see chapter 3.

36. Goléa, *Rencontres*, 162.

37. Eduard Hanslick, *Music Criticisms 1846–99*, trans. Henry Pleasants (Baltimore: Penguin, 1963), 217.

38. Gottfried Weber, *Gottfrieds von Strassburg Tristan und die Krise des hochmittelalterlichen Weltbildes um 1200*, 2 vols. (Stuttgart: J. B. Metzler, 1953), 1:87, as quoted in translation by Joseph Campbell, *The Masks of God: Creative Mythology* (New York: Viking, 1968), 241–42.

39. Claude Rostand, *Olivier Messiaen* (Paris: Ventadour, 1957), 36.

40. See H. W. Janson, *Apes and Ape Lore in the Middle Ages and the Renaissance* (London: Warburg Institute, 1952), 29 and *passim*.

41. Goléa, *Rencontres*, 165.

42. Tanneguy de Quénetain, "Messiaen, Poet of Nature," *Music and Musicians* 11 (May 1963): 10.

43. Olivier Messiaen, Preface, *Vingt regards sur l'enfant Jésus* (Paris: Durand, 1957), ii; see also Robert Sherlaw Johnson, *Messiaen* (London: J. M. Dent, 1975), 41–42.

44. Ferguson, *Signs and Symbols in Christian Art*, 154.

45. The Balinese monkey chant is sung by a large number of men, who perform the song of the monkey armies that appear to rescue Princess Sita from a demon king in the *Rāmāyana*; see Michael Tenzer, *Balinese Music* (Berkeley and Singapore: Periplus Editions, 1991), 98–99. The resemblance is noted by Johnson, *Messiaen*, 81, but without discussion.

46. Jonathan Saville, *The Medieval Erotic Alba* (New York: Columbia University Press, 1972), 180.

47. See Johnson, *Messiaen*, 41.

48. Messiaen, Preface, *Vingt regards*, ii.

49. Johnson, *Messiaen*, 81.

50. Messiaen, *The Technique of My Musical Language*, 1:17.

51. David Preiser's translation in his notes to the compact disk *Harawi* issued by Koch International (KIC-CD-7292).

52. The painting, sometimes identified by an alternate name, *Seeing Is Believing*, was lost during World War II and, according to Penrose (personal letter of 19 July 1973), was not found after the war. See also Goléa, *Rencontres*, 169, and Johnson, *Messiaen*, 100. Messiaen told me in conversation that he had never seen the actual painting.

53. Messiaen understood her "missing" body probably to be "continued in the sky" (Goléa, *Rencontres*, 169, as quoted in translation by Griffiths, *Olivier Messiaen and the Music of Time*, 126).

54. I quote from the translation by Barbara Reynolds, in Dante Alighieri, *La Vita Nuova* (Harmondsworth: Penguin, 1969), 60–61.

55. I quote for convenience from Gottfried von Strassburg, *Tristan*, trans. A. T. Hatto (Baltimore: Penguin, 1960), 198, 204.

56. D'Harcourt and d'Harcourt, *Les Musique des Incas*, 2:467.

57. Gerardus van der Leeuw, *Religion in Essence and Manifestation*, trans. J. E. Turner, 2 vols. (New York: Harper and Row, 1963), 2:374.

58. Ibid., 2:375; see also Kathi Meyer-Baer, *The Music of the Spheres and the Dance of Death* (Princeton: Princeton University Press, 1963), *passim*.

59. Goléa, *Rencontres*, 170.

60. Messiaen would seem to have been intellectually intrigued by astrology, though he did not take it seriously as a guide to life. He took a special delight in the fact that his first and undoubtedly best class in composition recognized that he was a Sagittarian and called themselves his "flèches" (Samuel, *Entretiens*, 196; Mari, *Olivier Messiaen*, 40).

61. See Buñuel, *L'Age d'Or and Un Chien Andalou*, 96, 109.

62. See the star map dated 1776 in Robert H. Baker, 7th ed. *Astronomy* (Princeton: Van Nostrand, 1959), 20.

63. Goléa, *Rencontres*, 170.

64. For information about the Tibetan Buddhist mantra, I am indebted to Robert Shafer.

65. According to Jane Manning, however, "Messiaen's endearing long-standing fascination and affinity with birds and their song may perhaps provide the key to what seems an astonishing grasp of the mechanics of the female voice" ("The Songs and Song Cycles," in *The Messiaen Companion*, ed. Hill, 105).

3

Turangalîla-symphonie: The Cosmic Dimension of Love

The ten-movement *Turangalîla-symphonie*, the middle work in Messiaen's Tristan trilogy, is also its largest, being scored for orchestra with the piano given a particularly striking solo role.[1] The piano passages stretch the performer to the utmost, for they are a *tour de force* of pianistic techniques—chords, tone clusters, arpeggios, and massive trills consisting of juxtapositions of four-note clusters in the left hand played against four-note clusters in the right. Messiaen commented that because the piano writing is of such importance and requires such virtuosity and power, the symphony can be called "almost a piano concerto."[2] This instrument is used not only to introduce bird song elements, familiar from *Harawi*, but also to combine with the celesta, glockenspiel, and vibraphone to produce the *effect* of a gamelan, though without the precise sound that we would expect of the Balinese ensemble. Another unusual instrument, the ethereal Ondes Martenot, is also added and given some striking solo passages. This sweetly high-pitched electronic instrument carries the important theme of love in the symphony, and its sound is unearthly, seemingly timeless, and mystical. There is, however, no text except for the composer's detailed program notes, and there are no singers. The work's "collective effect," Malcolm Hayes has observed, "is of a quite unprec-

edented tumult of orchestral voices, which still has the power to discon-
cert and thrill that it must have had in 1949."[3]

The symphony, which is not organized according to sonata-allegro
form, utilizes its special arrangement of the instruments of the orchestra
to achieve the desired effects of tone color. Once the introductory matter
has been completed, each movement is structured to express the particular ideational content with which Messiaen has invested it. The story
of Tristan and Iseult is subjected to examination in the music, but we
will see that this narrative has been reduced to what the composer con-
siders to be the essentials: the emotional and transcendental realities that
make the love experience of these lovers at once unique and universal.
The experience is frankly sensual, as Messiaen himself admitted, and
autobiographical, as he was less willing to admit. In this work he had at
his disposal a vastly different and more flexible palette of tones and
colors than in *Harawi*, which, of course, utilizes only voice and piano.
Hence *Turangalîla-symphonie* is capable of probing the emotional depth
of the love experience in a manner that is more strikingly moving and
more accessible than in the case of the song cycle that forms Part I of
the Tristan trilogy. However, as Paul Griffiths has commented, "Ultimately, . . . the work is not made to be understood, but made rather to
draw its listeners through mind-defying complexity, alterations of time
sense and sheer brilliance into a state of amazement."[4]

Messiaen's point of departure in *Turangalîla-symphonie* is expressed in
his title, which he borrowed from the term that Śarṅgadeva uses to des-
ignate one of his 120 *talas*.[5] The term is made up of two Sanskrit words,
turanga and *lîla*. As his title suggests, Messiaen here was using musical
ideas and other material from Eastern music and Hindu thought somewhat as he had used Peruvian material in his song cycle *Harawi*. In the
program notes that he wrote for the symphony, he identified *lîla* as
"play" in a cosmic sense—that is, "of creation, of destruction, of recon-
struction, the play of life and death." But he also understood *lîla* as
"Love." On the other hand, *Turanga* "is time that runs, like a galloping
horse" and "that flows, like sand in an hourglass . . . movement and
rhythm." The word *Turangalîla* hence implies "love song, hymn to joy,
time, movement, rhythm, life and death" simultaneously.[6] Thus Messiaen's definition of *lîla* seems to be congruent with the Indian Shaivite
explanation of the meaning of the cosmic dance of the Lord Shiva. According to Ananda Coomaraswamy, the dance represents the Lord
Shiva's five activities, which include creation and destruction as well as
preservation, embodiment, and salvation.[7] And for the Vedānta school,

Turangalîla-symphonie 65

"the motive of creation was explained . . . as the 'sport' (*lîla*) of the World Soul, and the creation of the cosmos was thought of on the analogy of the production of a work of art from the mind of an artist."[8] Thus Messiaen uses the cosmic dance not only as a symbol of the lovers' transcending "frenetic dance of joy," but also as a symbol for his life as creator and for the *Turangalîla-symphonie* as a whole.

Of course, for Messiaen *lîla* is not just the cosmic dance in any mechanical sense, for it is given its energy by *love*. As Messiaen has said, "*Lîla* is also Love"—a statement that demonstrates his awareness of another important aspect of Hindu thought that is normally expressed through the myth of Krishna and the *gopîs*. The story is that as the lad Krishna was playing the flute, he attracted a number of *gopîs* or cow girls. He at first reproached them for neglecting their work and their husbands, but then he smiled at them and invited them to dance. This famous and erotic dance is known as *Krishna-lîla*.[9] From among the dancing *gopîs*, the god then chooses one, whose name is Rādhā, and takes her away. Later she will be his favorite. Her place in Indian mythology has been explained as follows: "She is the beloved favorite of Krishna who has known him since childhood. . . . Rādhā has always been the beloved of Krishna (in all their previous existences); they are really the same— the difference between them is only verbal, and Krishna created Rādhā for *lîla*."[10] *Lîla*—dance, love, delight—is hence central to Messiaen's analysis of a love which brings lovers together and unites them.

Equally important as the concept of *lîla* for Messiaen is *turanga*, which, as we have seen, was interpreted by him as time, movement, rhythm. It has been noted that the composer seems in his music to have been in revolt against modern pressures of chronological time and that he seemed to be seeking for an eternal, timeless state. Thus his references to "the time that runs, like a galloping horse" and "time that flows, like sand in an hourglass" appear to be a recognition of the tyranny of time to which he will not submit. Time may run or even fly, but it is possible through music to descend into an interior timelessness. Messiaen achieved this feat through playing with time and duration. For example, in the first movement of *Turangalîla-symphonie*, he has provided an extended rhythmic pattern in the strings that is run through thirteen times, while in the other four groups of instruments four other rhythmic patterns are being presented. The constancy of one pattern and its pull-and-tug on the other patterns are scarcely audible to the listener's ear; the auditor at first receives the impression that there is no beat, no time at all, only the natural pulsation of heartbeat and slow breathing. Far re-

moved from Western life, which is oriented to the clock and to the production of goods, such effects were derived by Messiaen from the Indian
talas systematized in Indian music theory and described by Śarṅgadeva.
In *Turangalîla-symphonie*, the composer especially uses the *rāgavardhana*
rhythm,[11] which, like his nonretrogradable rhythms, is the same whether
it is used in direct or retrograde fashion.

The cosmic dance, the play of creation, love, time, and movement, are
thus each important components of this symphony. But underlying it all
is the medieval love story that Wagner made "modern" in his own time,
and that Messiaen chose as the mythic armature about which *Turangalîla-
symphonie*, like *Harawi* and *Cinq rechants*, was fashioned. In the crucial
fifth movement, Messiaen said that he was providing a musical equivalent for Tristan's words to Isolde: "If the whole world were here with
us, I would not see anyone but you." However, since these exact words
appear nowhere in Wagner's libretto, Messiaen must have been speaking
figuratively of the passage in Act 2, scene 2, in which Tristan and Isolde
say:

> O sink hernieder,
> Nacht der Liebe,
> gib Vergessen,
> daß ich lebe,
> nimm mich auf
> in deinen Schoß,
> löse von der Welt mich los![12]
>
> (O, near to us, night of passion,
> grant unknowingness even of life.
> Seize me on your bosom,
> give me freedom from the world!)

In the sixth movement, "Jardin du sommeil d'amour," the garden that
surrounds them is Tristan, and it is Iseult as well. In the eighth movement, Tristan-Iseult transcends the two lovers.[13] The garden of love's
sleep reminds us of the flowery bank on which the lovers sink down in
Wagner's music drama and also of the fruit and flower imagery of Hieronymus Bosch's painting *The Garden of Earthly Delights* (Figure 2, located
after Preface).[14]

The love potion, though not expressly represented in any of the themes
of the symphony, is indicated when Messiaen explained that the love

expressed in *Turangalîla-symphonie*, as in the other two parts of the trilogy, is a "fatal, irresistible" love. It transcends all things, denies anything external to its own emotion, and is represented by the love potion that is imbibed by the lovers.[15] For Messiaen, however, the love potion is a symbol of the couple's love but is not a cause of that love. In the nineteenth century, Wagner's use of the love potion was the topic of considerable discussion by music critics, including Ludwig Ehlert, Hans Hopfen, and, as we have seen, the eminent Eduard Hanslick. Ehlert particularly insisted that the love potion, since it robbed the lovers of their free will, removed motivation from the drama and made it into something undramatic. Hanslick further claimed that if it is only symbolic, as some defenders of Wagner wished it to be, then it is, in his opinion, either superfluous or lacking in drama. Hopfen's viewpoint was that, rather than being either symbolic or superfluous, "the confusion of two different drinks is actually a subject for comedy."[16] As a man with considerably more respect for myth than the nineteenth-century critics, Messiaen was not afraid to revive the love potion, which for him could never be construed as comic. It is symbolic, but not superfluous, since it constitutes a significant element in his symphony. The love potion is tied to the tritonal interval in Songs 7 ("Adieu") and 9 ("L'escalier redit, gestes du soleil") of *Harawi*, and also will appear in the fifth *rechant* of *Cinq rechants*. In *Turangalîla-symphonie*, both the tritone and the idea of the love potion are ever-present, though a linkage between them cannot at all times be assumed.

In Wagner's music drama as in the Celtic, Germanic, and French sources for the Tristan story, the beautiful Isolde/Iseult is the one who, along with her mother, has healed Tristan of the near-fatal wound he received in fighting the Morolt.[17] Following the mortal blow given Tristan by Melot after the discovery of the lovers by Mark and his men, the hero has gone to his father's castle in Brittany in the hope that he may recover from the wound. While Tristan sleeps in Act 3, scene 1, Kurwenal sadly watches and comments on the ability of Isolde to cure wounds:

> Erwachte er,
> wär's doch nur,
> um für immer zu verscheiden:
> erschien zuvor *die Ärztin* nicht,
> die einz'ge, die uns hilft.[18]

(If he were to awaken,
it would only be
to depart forever from us,
unless *the healer* appears,
the only one who can help us.)

For Messiaen, the roles of healer, as exemplified in Iseult, and of magician were linked. He compared his heroine to Viviane whom Merlin loved, to Yseult and her command of love potions, and to Edgar Allan Poe's Ligeia "ruling over death." She is to be regarded as an adept at magic: "Her eyes journey ... into the past ... into the future."[19] Strangely, these heroines are not completely wholesome, helpful, or always healing. Iseult/Isolde becomes an unlucky love for Tristan; Vivian, who is called Nimue by Malory and Niniane in earlier versions, imprisons Merlin;[20] Ligeia, in Poe's eerie story of the same name, returns from the dead to rob the narrator's second wife of her life. Thus, although the *bien aimée* "of water, of heaven, of time" in *Harawi* was able to mitigate the psychic wounds mentioned in the poems of the vocal cycle, there remains more than a trace of the problematical in the characteristics attributed to the heroine of the *Turangalîla-symphonie*; she is at once wonderful and frightening. It has been noted that the poems set to music in *Poèmes pour Mi* and *Chants de Terre et de Ciel* indicate physical relationships that had earlier seemed a source of terror for Messiaen. This earlier terror continues to crop up in *Turangalîla-symphonie* in connection with the story of Iseult, the heroine.

In addition to the Wagner opera, Poe's "Ligeia," and the Arthurian legend, there are several other literary and artistic works that Messiaen cited as influencing the imagery and symbolism of the symphony. The literary influences include the lovers in Shakespeare's *Romeo and Juliet*; a poem, "L'Union libre" (1931), by the surrealist poet André Breton; another short story by Poe, "The Pit and the Pendulum"; and the short story "La Venus d'Ille" by Prosper Mérimée. The composer referred to paintings of Marc Chagall in which the artist portrays either the wife flying down to meet the husband or both lovers flying off into space, and also the paintings of Bosch, particularly the *Garden of Earthly Delights* (Figure 2). In *Cinq rechants* the influence of Bosch's work will again appear prominently in the form of the striking image of the lovers encapsulated in the crystal ball—a detail from the centerpiece of the painter's famous triptych.

Such diverse references to literary works and paintings, while rich in

Turangalîla-symphonie 69

implication as programmatic sources for Messiaen's symphony, do suggest difficulties with regard to the creation of unity in his composition. The problems that he faced were similar to those encountered in *Harawi* but here were made more complicated by the lack of a text: (1) How is it possible to make musical equivalences for verbal and pictorial images in what is essentially a nonverbal form? And (2) how is it possible to compose a work that, though diverse in sources, is characterized by wholeness and coherence? The solutions obviously must be different from the twelve songs of *Harawi*, since there he could rely on the language of poetry to link his music with the meaning he wished to express. His approach in the symphony was to take a number of themes, which are melodic, harmonic, and rhythmic in nature; these then became the objective correlatives for his thoughts and feelings and also became attached to the literary and pictorial references described in his program notes. These program notes hence are extremely valuable evidence, showing how the music relates to the mythic armature and how his musical material is wrapped around it. In the symphony, Messiaen achieved new dimensions, for it is like a sculpture of gigantic proportions, perhaps reminiscent of one of the larger sculptures of Henry Moore, Barbara Hepworth, or Alexander Calder. In addition to the instrumental forces, there is greater length, since the symphony takes nearly an hour and a half to perform in concert. And there is new emphasis on development by means of extension rather than by elimination, the latter a technique much used in *Harawi*. Finally, there is a new energy, particularly in the fifth movement of the symphony, and it is an energy that builds up a momentum unusual even for Messiaen.

For his treatment of the Tristan and Iseult story in the symphony, the composer chooses the following "cyclic themes": (1) the "statue" theme; (2) the "flower," theme, (3) the theme of love; and (4) a theme that is simply a chord progression. There is also a pair of ascending and descending scale passages, proceeding in contrary motion from each other, known as "the fan." These themes are carefully listed in the catalogue provided by Messiaen in his program notes.[21] In the "statue" theme, he wanted the listener to be reminded of "that oppressive, terrifying brutality of Mexican ancient monuments," but more especially of the previously mentioned "Venus d'Ille" of the Prosper Mérimée story. In that story, an ancient Roman statue, representing the goddess Venus, is discovered. The finder's son, who plans to be married that afternoon, carelessly places the wedding ring on the statue's finger while he plays a game of tennis. He forgets the ring on the statue's finger, and thus is

70   Olivier Messiaen and the Tristan Myth

forced to improvise for a ring during the wedding ceremony. Later that
night, the bridegroom goes to retrieve his original ring. To his horror,
he finds that the statue has clenched her fist and will not relinquish the
ring. The next morning the bridegroom is found dead—crushed—and
with horrible wounds about his body. His bride, half mad with fright,
relates the events of the previous night as she recalls them. She had gone
up to her room to await her husband. She felt a heavy weight sink down
in bed beside her, and then she heard her husband come into the room
and also enter the bed. The story continues:

> She heard a stifled cry. The person who was in bed beside her sat
> up, and seemed to stretch out both arms in front. Then she turned
> her head . . . and saw, so she says, her husband on his knees by the
> bed, with his head on a level with the pillow, in the arms of a sort
> of greenish giant who was embracing him with all its might. She
> said . . . that she recognized . . . can you guess? The bronze Venus,
> Monsieur de Peyrehorade's statue.[22]

The girl loses consciousness at this point. When she awakens, her eyes
meet the statue, "motionless, its legs and the lower half of its body on
the bed, the bust and arms stretched out before it, and in its arms her
lifeless husband."[23] Thus the theme of the statue in *Turangalîla-symphonie*
is laden with connotations of fear, awfulness, and dread—feelings previously stressed by Messiaen in Song 2 ("Bonjour toi, colombe verte")
and portions of Song 9 ("L'escalier redit, gestes du soleil") of *Harawi*. For
Messiaen, the statue theme was a wise choice in connection with the
love-death motif implicit in the Tristan story, but it also functions as a
figure of Conscience standing over the lover.

    To convey the idea of the terrifying statue, Messiaen chooses a se-
quence of six chords (made up of major and minor thirds, doubled). As
the composer has noted, the theme is usually performed by the trombones *fortissimo*[24] and consists of major and minor thirds that pass
through various key centers. The thirds are as follows: a major third built
on G♭, a major third built on C♭, a minor third built on B♮, a minor third
built on A♯, a major third on C, and a return to the first major third on
G♭. In Example 3.1, the trombones are joined by the tuba. These remind
one of the two chords, one based on an A♭ major seventh and the other
based on a dominant seventh in C major, which are played in quick
succession to mark the beginning of the Coronation Scene in Mussorgsky's *Boris Godunov* (Example 3.2). The apparent echo from the opera

Example 3.1

Boris Godunov is fitting not only because of the musical similarities or even because of Messiaen's long partiality to the opera[25] but also because the character of Boris is conscience-ridden and unhappy. Also, the statue theme in *Turangalîla-symphonie* recalls yet another statue that is connected with conscience: even though the chords in the passage dealing with the Commendatore's returning to take Don Giovanni to hell in Mozart's *Don Giovanni* are much more stationary than these, the feeling of terror is still congruent with the effect that Messiaen desired his own "statue" theme to have.

This heavy theme is contrasted with the airy lightness of the "flower" theme; here Messiaen said that he was especially thinking of the orchid,

Example 3.2

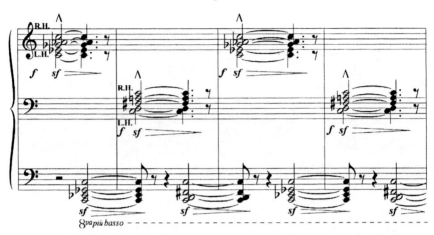

the fuchsia, the "red gladiolus," and the "excessively pliant convolvulus" or corn lily.[26] Each of these flowers is of the violet-red, blue, or red colors that the composer listed among his favorites. We may recall his frequent references to the beloved in *Harawi* as being "of fruit" and "of flower," especially in Song 7 ("Adieu toi"). For Messiaen, then, the "flower" theme was connected inextricably to the beloved and gives to the beloved all the qualities of fruitfulness, beauty, and decorativeness. Further, we know that he preferred nature and natural things to the artificiality of modern civilization; hence, while the "statue" theme is terrifying in its presentation of an object made by man, the "flower" theme, which reasserts nature, has connotations that are positive and also pleasant. Musically, this theme is composed of two melodic lines that move in opposite directions, the upper voice moving downward by means of step and leap, and the lower voice moving generally upward also by step and leap. The "flower" theme is one of great sweetness and simplicity; it is first played by English horn and clarinets so softly as to sound muted (Example 3.3a). The theme is repeated by the clarinets, then taken up by flute and bassoon, again played very softly (Example 3.3b). The composer compares the two melodic lines to two "eyes," important images in his poetry, especially in Song 1 of *Harawi*, where the lovers' glances are as if knit together ("sans denouer regards, toi").

The theme of love, although not described in any detail by Messiaen, was said by him to be of the very greatest importance,[27] as one would expect in a trilogy based on the Tristan story. However, the theme itself

Example 3.3a

Example 3.3b

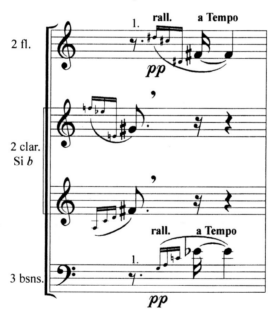

is not very complex. It weaves in and out of the tonality, sometimes touching on scalar degrees related to the tonal center; the strings provide a constant F♯ major tonal background. As noted, the theme is played slowly and thus gives the effect of being drawn out interminably. It has an ethereal calm because of its unhurried tempo and the lack of jagged

Example 3.4a
"More sinuous theme": Question

Example 3.4b
"More sinuous theme": Answer

Example 3.4c
Straightforward version

rhythms. The Ondes Martenot, with its "expressive and super-high" sound,[28] is chosen to carry the theme. The theme has two forms, a more sinuous form (Examples 3.4a and 3.4b) and a more straightforward one (Example 3.4c). There are ingenious variants of both forms of the theme that appear throughout the symphony.

The final theme is not a single theme but several emanations of chords—sometimes enchaining, sometimes descending or ascending—and they may be tossed off lightly or given heavy, ponderous treatment. They appear most prominently in the piano solo in the eighth movement (Example 3.5). Messiaen associated their shifting shapes with the adjurations of the alchemists to the magical substances with which they were working: "dissociate and coagulate."[29] The concepts of coagulation and disintegration are part of the ancient lore of alchemy, in which the sub-

Example 3.5

stances of sulphur and mercury were used to represent "the two basic generative forces."[30] Sulphur stands for Sun-King-Man, while mercury, known also as quicksilver, stands for Moon-Queen-Woman. "Alchemy," as a modern writer on the subject has noted, "is based on the view that man, as a result of the loss of his original 'Adamic' state, is divided within himself. He regains his integral nature only when the two powers, whose discord has rendered him impotent, are again reconciled with one another."[31] Hence the aim of alchemy is to integrate masculine with feminine forces. Symbolically this takes place in the chemical marriage of sulphur and mercury in the alchemical retort. There they come together and coagulate, the two elements becoming one compound. Carl Jung quotes a poem by an alchemist, "Merculinus," who describes the process of the masculine and feminine conjunction:

> White-skinned lady, lovingly joined to her ruddy-limbed
> husband,
> Wrapped in each other's arms in the bliss of connubial union,
> Merge and dissolve as they come to the goal of perfection:
> They that were two are made one, as though of one body.[32]

Messiaen's own creative method seems in line with alchemical processes in the way in which he took disparate but carefully selected elements and forged them together in his art. Furthermore, the conjunction of man and woman within a mystical experience may be said to be at the very heart of the symphony.

To generalize: Messiaen weaves statue, flower, love, and the chordal themes together with the ingenious use of Indian rhythms as well as even more intricate permutations of various rhythmic patterns. For each movement, the composer chooses one or more of the themes to bear the ideational content, then juxtaposes the themes skillfully with episodic material that prepares the way for the theme. His own poetic titles for the movements and his program notes not only explicate the movements, but also show the mythic design around which the musical material is wound as if around the armature of a piece of additive sculpture, as he had done in *Harawi*.

The structure of the entire symphony appears to fall neatly into a two-part division, with the first five movements making up one unit and the last five movements another. The first four provide a formalistic prelude to the fifth, which is a climactic point for the entire symphony. "Introduction," the first movement, juxtaposes the statue and flower themes, and this juxtaposition is further evidence of Messiaen's recognition that beauty and terror often appear side by side in life. The flower theme is heard again in the fourth movement, which follows a third that has emphasized rhythmic interest over the utilization of cyclic themes. The fifth movement, which closes the first half of the symphony, symbolizes the ecstatic central event of the love of the two lovers as well as their transcendence over time and earthly life.

The final five movements are a treatment of the fulfillment of the love. These do not, however, outline a straightforward line of progress upward; after the beautiful sixth movement, "Jardin du sommeil d'amour" ("Garden of Love's Sleep"), there is yet the terrifying seventh movement that Messiaen has associated with Poe's eerie story "The Pit and the Pendulum." The eighth movement, "Développement de l'amour" ("Development of Love"), also utilizes the statue theme and therefore is not completely removed from the element of terror. By the ninth movement, the terror has become exorcized, and the tenth movement ("Final") returns to the ecstasy of the fifth movement.

Turangalîla-symphonie 77

PART I

Movement 1 "Introduction"

The shape of the first movement is binary; there is an exposition of the first two main themes, statue and flower, followed by a second section that forms the body of this introductory movement. Between the two sections is a solo cadenza, characterized by arpeggios, thick chords, acciaccaturas, runs, and trills for the piano. At the beginning the audience will hear what Leonard Burkat has called "a commanding figure chiefly low in the strings"[33] that consists of leaping sixteenth notes in a mode approaching Messiaen's Mode 4. At measure 11 a resounding tam-tam crash is heard; then what Burkat has labeled "a quick call"[34] (measures 16–17) in English horn, horns, bassoons, and trombones precedes a descending whole tone scale marked by tritones in the piano, perfect fifths in the oboes, and major sixths in the clarinets, serving as preparation for the statue theme. But before the statue theme can appear, there is a glissando—erroneously anthropomorphized by Burkat as "a shriek"[35]—in the strings and Ondes Martenot and a massive trill by the piano that leads directly to the first entries of the statue, loud and terrifying as in Mérimée's "La Venus d'Ille" when the statue proceeds to lumber up the stairs and crush the life out of the bridegroom. Messiaen follows the terrifying statue theme with brilliant "jumbles of sound" (chromatics in groups of ten and twelve notes in a section marked *"bien modéré"*) that additionally heighten the mood of fear and suspense.

A *Presque vif* section ensues, in which the piano begins on a very high note (g#''') and descends by half steps, one finger of the left hand hitting next to one finger of the right hand all the way down the keyboard chromatically in thirty-second notes as the other instruments pursue independent paths in sixteenth-note values. When the piano reaches its nadir, another dramatic descent—by tritone (diminished fifths and augmented fourths) and perfect fourths—is begun on high by the winds and strings. Two chords reminiscent of Stravinsky's constructions lead to the delicate flower theme, first in the clarinets, next in the English horn, and finally in the flutes. Shifting tonal centers are used to represent the various colors of the flowers—the orchid, the fuchsia, the gladiolus, and the corn lily. The piano, vibraphone, and celesta break into the hushed atmosphere with softly chiming chords.

The cadenza is made up of one pattern after another, beginning with a linear passage of thirty-second notes in the right hand which is played

78   Olivier Messiaen and the Tristan Myth

against a pattern in the left hand that is staggered two notes ahead of the other to create an autonomous, yet coinciding sonority. The tempo is at first marked *lent*, then *bien modéré, modéré un peu vif, pressez, presque lent, lent, vif, un peu vif,* and *bien modéré.* Even at a slow tempo marking, the thirty-second notes create a very fast, even frantic speed. Although the composer claimed in his theoretical works that the term *polytonality* does not adequately describe his harmonic practice, he nevertheless admitted that music can be in "the atmosphere of several tonalities at once." This is expressed by the term *polymodality.* By means of "polymodality . . . we superpose our modes, and there again, we are present at the hatching of polytonal aggregations."[36] So also it is in this cadenza, which ultimately will swoop downward to very low, slow, heavy sounding chromatics that lead directly to the body of the movement.

In the body of the Introduction several rhythmic schemes are simultaneously played off against one another and with each other. The gamelan, for example, has an ostinato rhythm, while the strings' rhythm is based on the retrograde *rāgavardhana tala.* The various rhythmic schemes, each operating at different rates of speed while covering the same distance different numbers of times (for example, the strings complete their scheme thirteen and one-half times, while the cymbal goes through its scheme four and one-fifth times), weave in and out like iridescent threads in a medieval tapestry. In addition to these schemes, there are interludes where the piano and brass play alternately.

The structure of the movement is very clear, since the gamelan provides a constant element, which appears eight times, at its first two appearances equal in length but thereafter shrinking in length at each appearance until it is less than one measure long. Then it grows to seven measures, but at its final appearance it has now shrunk to a measure and a half. The piano-brass interludes appear between each of the gamelan sections. These constant factors, against the shifting modalities and rhythms of strings and woodwinds and against the growing and shrinking cymbal, create a movement that is both tightly ordered and yet timeless in effect. Perhaps David Drew's observation that Messiaen was searching for a music that expresses "a new Time and a new Space"[37] was not inaccurate. With a descent by tritone while the statue theme resounds—followed by a "fan" played by the piano simultaneously with a sliding descent by woodwinds and bassoons, four cymbal crashes and loud kettledrum beat—the movement comes to a close. Its purpose has been to serve as preparation for the second movement, "Chant d'amour 1," and also for the remaining movements of the symphony. The fan also had a special meaning for Messiaen, who was attracted to "two symmetrically inverse figures framing a neutral central motif," as in designs on Gothic and Romanesque churches.[38]

Movement 2: "Chant d'amour 1"

A "Song of Love" without a text, the second movement apparently reflects the notion that some thoughts are too deep for words and that only music is capable of conveying them. This idea was given credence by Felix Mendelssohn in his *Songs without Words*, but a more direct precedent for Messiaen is Hector Berlioz's *Roméo et Juliette*, which, to be sure, intersperses orchestral music with choral passages. However, at the most significant part of the work, the declaration of love between Romeo and Juliet, Berlioz chose orchestral sounds alone to express their feelings: text and vocal music are eschewed in favor of pure expression of emotion in the sounds of the instrumental music of the orchestra.

There are no specific program notes to tell us precisely what Messiaen was thinking at each point in "Chant d'amour 1." It is possible, however, to see analogies with the text for *Harawi*, and also the composer's title for this movement is directly suggestive of material in Wagner's *Tristan und Isolde*. In both *Harawi* and Wagner's music drama, as we have seen, the lovers are observed out of doors with their eyes entwined in rapturous gazes. Further, hints may be derived from the fifth movement of *Turangalîla-symphonie*, where Messiaen indicated explicitly that in his presentation of love he was thinking in part of Romeo and Juliet, for whom each was the other's entire world. Finally, material from *Cinq rechants*, where the lovers fly off into space, may be relevant, since for Messiaen the experience of love was something exalting and transcending.

The structure of the second movement reveals further elements of the treatment of love as derived from the Tristan story. The thematic material emphasizes the cyclic theme of love played by the Ondes Martenot—a lush theme that moves in and out of the tonal framework of F♯ major. The symbolism is clear, for although this theme more often than not departs from its tonal center, the pedal chords in F♯ major in the strings and woodwinds establish it, like love itself, as grounded in a stable relationship. In addition, there are two trumpet motifs that are not related to any of the cyclic themes. These provide sharp contrast to the sweet, calm theme of love, for they are in turn raucous, teasing, and even harsh. The juxtaposition of the two themes is reminiscent of the tenets of Surrealism, which insists on impossibilities or on at least the reconciliation of opposites. Two moods are thus set in opposition in this movement, just as in real life human beings are often torn between two states of mind.

The musical form involves, as Messiaen indicated, the use of refrain (repeated after the first couplet), two couplets, and a development. In addition, there is a short introduction to begin the movement, and a final codalike reminder of the refrain to close it. The refrain and couplet form will be exploited to a far greater extent in the third part of the trilogy, *Cinq rechants*, and will be examined in connection with that work in the next chapter. As used in the second movement of *Turangalîla-symphonie*, the form is shaped by a number of influences, among them the prime one being the alternation of *chant* and *rechant* as in Claude le Jeune's *Le Printemps*, a posthumous collection of *chansons* published in 1603.[39] But there may also be influence from the medieval rondeau with its repeated refrain; further, there may be some influence from Couperin's organ masses, which contain episodes called couplets. Wilfrid Mellers has described the latter: "Couperin's couplets on the Kyrie, Gloria, Offertory, Benedictus (Elevation), Sanctus, and Agnus Dei have, like those of his contemporaries, mostly lost their connection with the plainsong base; they are short pieces, headed by a phrase of the Latin text, some in the old fugal idiom, others more operatic in technique."[40] However, Messiaen's work differs significantly from any of his possible models or sources, as his inclusion of a development section will demonstrate.

The beginning of the movement is marked by loud, disjunctive, and extremely dissonant chords. Thereafter an insistent thrumming is produced, first by the snare drum, and subsequently by each group of instruments striking C♯ in various octaves in turn. This then leads to the refrain, which is made up of one of the trumpet motifs and the theme of love. The trumpet motif here is a teasing, Gershwinesque tune, which proceeds throughout the three trumpets, strings, and winds, sometimes hocketing as it leaps from trumpet to trumpet. It moves by half step and by leap, moving in and out of an F♯ tonal center. Although there are many meanderings away from F♯, the final notes nevertheless place the motif within the context of this tonal center.

Shortly, however, the melody will fly out of the tonality to outline a descending C major triad before returning to the sound of a dominant seventh chord (see Example 3.4a: "More sinuous theme: Question" earlier in this chapter). This portion of the theme functions as a kind of "question," ending as it does on the fifth of the tonality. The "answer" begins lower and does not soar quite as high as the question; it too begins outside of the tonality but ends on the key note F♯ after going through a number of nonharmonic tones. Its pedal chord is the tonic in F♯ major (see Example 3.4b: "More sinuous theme: Answer"). The weaving in and out of the tonal center gives the melody a sensuous, seductive quality and a delicious ambiguity, which is heightened by the slow tempo in eight-note values, as opposed to the fast and teasing trumpet motif in sixteenth notes. Again there is the juxtaposition of the two modes—the serious, even ponderous one of love, and the lighter, brighter one of the trumpet.

The first couplet is introduced by glissandos in the Ondes Martenot over soft *pizzicato* and *col legno* strings and is alternated with a chromatic motif in two parts, played by flutes and bassoons. The second couplet again utilizes two motifs. The first motif, played by the oboes and English horn, has a melody in chromatic steps and is "harmonized" by the interval of a perfect fourth. The parallel fourths, moving stepwise, have a distinct sound and are separable from the rest of the harmonies occurring simultaneously. There are changing meters encompassing 2/8, 7/16, 4/8, 3/8, and 2/4 metrical divisions within an eleven-measure span.

The development that comes after the refrains and couplets takes the trumpet motif from the refrain and elongates it by constant repetition, extending a motif of a few notes for twenty-five measures. Then the same motif is fragmented and tossed around. More fragmented intervals are heard, as the entire development builds up to an immensely slow statement of the theme of love from the refrain, this time in the Ondes Martenot, brass, and woodwinds, heavily weighted with chords. Both trumpet themes are heard in fragmentation, then a final fragment of melody from the Ondes is heard, which seems like a variation on the "answer" portion of the theme of love outlining as it does the first and fifth scale steps of the key of F♯ major (Example 3.6). The familiar descending closing formula is played by piano and strings, followed by a drum beat that ends the movement.

Movement 3: "Turangalîla 1"

Also a "Hymn to Joy" and a time play, "Turangalîla 1" uses three themes—one in the solo clarinet and the Ondes Martenot; another in the bassoons, trombones, gamelan, and piano; and a third in the oboes and flutes—which may be likened to three *dramatis personae* that alternately

Example 3.6

take the stage. Messiaen also pointed out that there is a fourth "theme," which is chordal in character. Two moods are present in the movement, one of calmness and coolness created by slower tempi and softer dynamics, and another more passionate and established by a slightly faster tempo and louder dynamics. The complex rhythmic schemes include paired augmentations and diminutions in the horns and violoncellos, augmentations and diminutions in the percussion instruments, and a rhythmic canon in the oboe and flute. Of particular interest is the wide-ranging third theme, which belongs to the first flute and first oboe. It has dissonant intervallic leaps, played as a retrograde rhythmic canon. Both the melody and the rhythmic pattern take twelve measures to run through the forward and retrograde versions of the canon, with the crossing of the two patterns occurring at the end of the sixth measure and the beginning of the seventh. Beginning in this section and continuing almost to the close of the movement is the rhythmic "theme," which is as follows: the maracas, which Messiaen designated as "mineral," at first diminishes and then "increases" (is augmented); the drum, which he calls "animal," at first "increases" (is augmented) and then diminishes; while the woodblock, termed "vegetable," remains the same.[41] An ostinato in parallel octaves is played by the gamelan as an accompaniment to the flute and oboe soli. A final *bien modéré* section follows, and finally there is a return to the initial tempo. The final statement is from the woodblocks, beating a long-short-short-short-long rhythm, accompanied by the soft pizzicato of the contrabass.

Movement 4: "Chant d'amour 2"

A greater interest in formal design seems to dominate in the fourth movement, "Chant d'amour 2," which has been described as having a "simultaneous multilayering of rhythmically, timbrally, and harmonically disjunct strands of material to assemble a kind of heterophonic 'mobile.'"[42] The general plan for the movement is that of scherzo and trio but with considerable variation on this form, in this case having nine sections:

1. Scherzo (piccolo and bassoon); rhythmic theme (woodblock).
2. Bridge.
3. Refrain, trio no. 1 (woodwinds).
4. Trio no. 2 (string soloists).
5. Trio no. 1 and trio no. 2 (woodwinds and strings) in superposition, with bird songs (piano).
6. Bridge.
7. Reprise, superposition of scherzo, two trios, and "statue" theme. These are all presented simultaneously.
8. Cadenza (piano solo).
9. Coda, with clarinets playing "flower" theme *pianissimo*, three trombones playing "statue" theme *fortissimo*, refrain by the Ondes and solo violins.[43]

This does not mean that Messiaen parts company completely with the traditional scherzo, succinctly described by Willi Apel as characterized by a "rapid tempo in 3/4 meter, vigorous rhythm, a certain abruptness of thought involving elements of surprise and whim, and a kind of bustling humor that ranges from the playful to the sinister."[44] Messiaen's scherzo theme has a staccato, leaping melody with abrupt starts and stops, played in widely spaced octaves by the piccolo and bassoon. Beneath the melodic theme, the woodblock beats out its rhythmic theme. The piano enters, and its arpeggios, added to the melody, create jumbles of sound. The bridge that follows is likewise remarkable in that it concludes with a tremendous stepwise "fan," which opens outward instead of closing in as it leads to the refrain and the first trio. In the next repetition of the bridge, the fan closes.

When the theme of love appears in this movement, it has fewer inter-

Example 3.7

vallic echoes from its use in earlier instances; yet in the similarity of contour and also in its weaving in and out of the tonal center, there is once again a kind of aural or psychological identity with its previous appearances (Example 3.7). The bird songs used in section 5 of this movement contrast with their previous use in *Harawi* in that here they are barred, unlike the wild, free treatment in the song cycle, but they are again characterized by many fast notes—that is, by groups of five, six, and seven thirty-second notes. Concerning his use of bird songs, however, Messiaen observed that he had to adapt their fast tempi, high pitches, and microtones for playing by modern musical instruments.[45]

The terrifying statue theme, which has not appeared since the first movement, comes back in the seventh section, which also contains a reprise of the scherzo theme and both trios. This section, instead of coming to a close, simply halts on an unresolved harmony. After a rest begins the piano cadenza, which eschews all the devices used in the first cadenza in this movement. The coda opens with the flower theme, followed by the massive trill borrowed from the first movement when the statue theme is introduced *fortissimo*. To close the movement, the piano begins an arpeggiated added sixth chord on A. Drew has noted that the added sixth was somewhat of an obsession with Messiaen; further, he perceptively has observed that it is " 'the inhibitory degree *par excellence*', because in an odd way it is half concord and half discord. The consonance and dissonance exist side by side, in a state of mutual frustration. Thus the added sixth satisfies Messiaen's need for musical materials that subvert the traditional tension-relaxation pattern, and hence alter the relationship of the music to the time factor."[46] Clearly Messiaen's choice of an added sixth, which seems to roll on and on upward, is another means of destroying time and asserting the eternally transcendent in his music.

Movement 5: "Joie du sang des étoiles"

Everything thus far in the symphony may be seen as prelude to the fifth movement, the title of which is translated as "Joy of the Stars' Blood." During the first four movements, their formal schemes have shifted and thus have created a kaleidoscopic effect of designs perhaps reminiscent of the shapes seen in art identified with Synthetic Cubism. Now that the meaning of the symphony has reached its crisis in the fifth movement, it seems to burst forth into something more spectacular in its project of applying music to the Tristan myth. Not surprisingly, Messiaen connected the movement with the cosmic dance of the lovers (discussed in connection with Song 11, "Katchikatchi les étoiles," of *Harawi*); with the love of Romeo and Juliet, but not with the tragic aspects of that love; and, most importantly, with the love of Tristan and Iseult.[47] The composer also indicated that important aspects of this movement are revealed through reference to André Breton's poem "L'Union Libre" ("Free Union"), a sensuous panegyric on the physical qualities of the poet's wife. Messiaen essentially uses one musical theme for this movement, a variant of the statue theme, now not ponderous, heavy, and terrifying, but lightly leaping and joyous in mood. All associations with "La Venus d'Ille" have now vanished. However, he also brings back the original form of the statue theme and adds new rhythmic interest to it.

In contrast to its use in *Harawi*, the cosmic dance is present in an upward bounding theme, replicating the movements of a wild, leaping dance by lovers who have transcended time and earthly boundaries. Following Messiaen's suggestion in his program notes,[48] this idea may be extended by reference to Chagall's *The Red Sun* (1949), painted shortly after Messiaen had finished his symphony but nevertheless supplying a gloss on its meaning since the composer was familiar with similar subject matter in this painter's work. Werner Schmalenbach has commented:

Again and again in Chagall's pictures these couples appear—lovers, betrothed, newlywed. They leave the ground and soar up in the heavens, the effusiveness of their feelings defying the law of gravity. So has he celebrated Love in countless paintings, countless re-groupings. . . . Before the red arc of the sun, the girl floats up in a dress of dreamy blue to meet her betrothed with his yellow suit, yellow face and green hair. The surrounding figures and objects share their joy . . . the flying violinist . . . flowers, flowers.[49]

So too the expansiveness of the lovers' mood is evidenced in Messiaen's quotation from Juliet's words in his program notes: "My bounty is as boundless as the sea" (*Romeo and Juliet* 2.2.133). The composer also quoted the alleged words of Tristan to Iseult: "If the whole world were visible to us at once, I would see nothing but you."[50] To be sure, during the love-duet of Act 2, scene 2, of Wagner's opera, there are passages sung by both of the lovers which express this kind of preoccupation with one another to the exclusion of the world around them:

> bricht mein Blick sich wonn'erblindet,
> erbleicht die Welt
> mit ihrem Blenden. . . .[51]

> (Dazzled eyes are sealed by bliss,
> the world with its adornments becomes pale.)

Such a love not only encompasses all things but also paradoxically is willing to abjure everything—world, sea, time, space, and other persons.

In this context, the connotations implied in the imagery of the "stars' blood" must be seen as mixed, for here again we are reminded that stars for Messiaen were symbolic of the spirit, but blood (red) represents passion, suffering—the liturgical color for martyrdom. Quite simply stated in this regard, the lovers' physical passion has a spiritual aspect as well. But there is an aspect of musical imagery too, since stars are often found in clusters, which, like blood or musical structure, appear to disintegrate and reintregrate—or in the words of the alchemical formula that Messiaen liked to quote, they "coagulate and disintegrate." In alchemical terms, we are reminded of the formula that stands for the reconciliation of masculine and feminine elements.[52]

But it is perhaps Messiaen's allusion to Breton's "L'Union Libre" that places all the other imagery into perspective. In this poem Breton speaks sensuously of his wife's great power over him:

> Ma femme à la chevelure de feu de bois
> Aux pensées d'éclairs de chaleur

> (My beloved with woodfire hair
> With thoughts like flashes of heat lightning.)[53]

In the conclusion of the poem she is "Ma femme . . . /Aux yeux de niveau d'eau de niveau d'air de terre et de feu" ("Woman of mine . . . /

Example 3.8

Reduction from score

With water-level eyes the level of air earth and fire"). The beloved for Breton—and for Messiaen as well—is so basic to life as to be comparable to the four basic alchemical elements: the beloved *is* Earth, Water, Fire, and Air. Breton's poem portrays his beloved in strongly physical terms: "Aux bras d'écume de mer et d'écluse" ("arms of sluice and sea foam"), "aux aisselles de martre et de fênes" ("armpits of marten and beechnut"), "la langue d'ambre" ("tongue of rubbed amber"). The implication here is that Messiaen too was celebrating the physical as well as the spiritual. Thus as Goléa has commented with reference to the symphony, "The amorous language of Messiaen, expressed thus in music, is true to the sense of erotic sculptures of India, entirely lacking hypocrisy, and even approaching shamelessness."[54] Like the statues of lovers on the temple at Konārak in India, the erotic becomes symbolic of rejoicing and mystical experience.[55]

In the exposition of this movement of the symphony, the composer still uses the "statue" theme, retaining the interval of the third in its first part or *a* section; then in the *b* section the theme moves to a lower pitch and finally leaps upward as it initiates a small excursion. Once both parts of the theme have been heard, the exposition closes with a fan with the woodwinds, brass, and strings carrying the descending tones and the piano carrying the ascending ones (in this case, a whole-tone scale). Ultimately there will be a triple exposition with variation form, followed by a development, piano cadenza, and coda. Of particular interest are the "hurled intervals," which consist of minor sixth, diminished fifths, and minor seconds, all of which continue the leaping motion that is so prominent in this movement. The variation is a strident, insistent motif in the brass and winds that consists essentially of four repeated chords. The chords to a large extent are superposed minor seconds, mixed with major seconds of clusters of adjacent tones (Example 3.8). The third

Example 3.9

Reduction from score

chord has a cluster in the center, consisting of a G♭, A♭, and A♮. The rhythm also adds to the insistent quality: There is yet one more set of hurled chords, capped by four chords that have a suspiciously jazzy flavor, each separate from the other by the space of a measure (Example 3.9). These chords, along with the excitement generated by the whole movement, lend credence to Wilfrid Mellers's comment on the relationship between *Turangalîla-symphonie* and jazz: "In this work the corybantic fast movements are significantly allied to the new-old primitivism of jazz both in the hypnotic repetitiveness of their riffs and breaks and in the blatantly scored juiciness of their harmony."[56]

While in the development the joyous theme is fragmented and is otherwise transformed by modulation and key change, the original statue theme is brought back in the horns, trumpets, and trombones. But while this theme is being played, the woodwinds play the joyous statue theme, and the strings pursue an independent chromatic path; the gamelan keeps up a steady ostinato, which adds to the already thick texture.

But it is the tremendous physical energy of the fifth movement that separates it from other works by Messiaen and that even sets it apart from other movements of the same symphony. Drew has commented: "Not since the *Alleluia* of *L'Ascension* has Messiaen been influenced by the dance, and never before have the quantitative rhythms possessed such kinetic force. Everything, from the wonderfully varied orchestration to the close-knit cellular structure . . . contributes to the accumulation of a tension almost too great to bear."[57] Thereupon Drew cogently notes how the tension is resolved and how the cadenza, based on the thirds of the original statue theme, is brought in:

> At the climax, five *fortissimo* chords deflect the impetus of the music, and its entire force is thrown into a cadenza for the piano.

Although the piano has nothing but the bare thirds of the cyclic theme in the semiquaver rhythm in which they have been heard throughout, the instrument seems, in some unaccountable way, to have been invested with a force greater than that of the orchestra. It is as if the *fortissimo* chords had brought about some kind of nuclear fission—indeed, in a strictly musical sense they have. The rhythmic nucleii are disintegrated and there is nothing left but for the music to return to its most elemental state—the cyclic theme. Its re-statement, in a new harmonic guise, after the piano's wild cadenza, is the natural conclusion to the movement.[58]

The close comes on a long-held tonic chord with an added sixth. The cosmic dance, which reflects at once the physical and mystical expression of love, has come to a close. The lovers will now sleep in the Garden of Love's Sleep.

PART II

Movement 6: "Jardin du sommeil d'amour"

The "Garden of Love's Sleep," which opens the second half of the symphony, might be considered a continued fulfillment of the love celebrated in the previous movements. In this movement, all is idyllic, but it will not be possible for this state to continue indefinitely. Thus the seventh movement will contain once again a descent into terror, apparently symbolizing the way that conscience threatens those who love and enjoy. The eight movement, "Développement de l'amour," will be a fairly straightforward link in the chain of fulfillment; nevertheless, there will be here too reminders of the terrifying statue theme. The ninth movement, "Turangalîla 3," will recall the calm and contemplative mood of "Turangalîla 1," its "mate" in the first part of the symphony, while the last movement, echoing the fifth, contains the final resolution of the entire work—the breaking forth into unmitigated joy.

The sixth movement, then, begins the progression toward the ultimate joy of its conclusion. The lovers are asleep in the "Garden of Love's Sleep." The music presents the greatest contrast possible with the movement that has immediately preceded it, since the fifth movement is noisy, boisterous, thick-textured, with busy, energetic rhythms and with a wild, leaping melodic line. Now the theme is a single one, and it is, according to Messiaen, the cyclic theme of love,[59] here adhering more closely to the

Example 3.10

F♯ major tonal center; on its second appearance, the ending consists of a leap downward from the third of the scale to the fifth below (Example 3.10). The tempo is slow, the dynamic level soft, and the texture extremely thin, even transparent. The scene is reminiscent of the bank of flowers on which Wagner's Tristan and Isolde recline and also of the fenced-in orchard behind the castle of Tintagel where, according to Bédier's redaction of the medieval sources, Tristan and Iseult were accustomed to meet. In that orchard were "numberless trees" with "fruit on them, birds and clusters of sweet grapes." Here Tristan and the queen kept their tryst, and it is said that "the night and the branches of the pine protected them."[60] Further source material for the garden scene in *Turangalîla-symphonie* may also be found in the famous grotto in the forest in Gottfried von Strassburg or the forest bower in Béroul; here King Mark finds the lovers asleep with a sharp sword placed between them.[61] In Béroul, the king looks at the lovers and muses: "I can well believe, if I have any sense, that if they loved each other wickedly they would certainly not be wearing clothes and there would be no sword between them. They would be lying together quite differently. I was intent on killing them, but now I shall not touch them."[62]

But no menacing figure threatens the lovers in the sixth movement, where fruit, flowers, and bird song are components of the imagery in the garden. The fruit imagery, uppermost in Messiaen's mind, must stem at least in part from Hieronymus Bosch's painting *The Garden of Earthly Delights* (Figure 2), especially the central panel, to which the composer will refer in the text of *Cinq rechants*. The flowers are certainly the fuchsia, gladiolus, and corn lily, previously noted by Messiaen in his introduction to the entire symphony, though in his notes to the sixth movement he also mentions "new" flowers, which he did not specify. But the flower theme that has previously been encountered will not be found here. Inevitably, however, bird songs are present here in the garden, identified by Messiaen as sung by a nightingale, a blackbird, and a "garden warbler." These bird songs are played by the piano, which creates an atonal embroidery over the tonal theme. In his gnomic way, Messiaen wrote, "All the birds of the stars," which is a backward glance at Song 10 of *Harawi*.[63] Once again birds and stars, both associated with transcendence, are linked to the lovers who themselves hence can be considered to be like heavenly bodies.

In his program notes accompanying the symphony, Messiaen wrote that the lovers are encapsulated in the sleep of love; out of them emerges a "landscape" that merges the two of them into a garden.[64] Thus now both lovers and not just the beloved encircle the fruit and flower imagery previously found in *Harawi*. In the symphony the lovers are united with each other and with nature. Through this transcendental experience, the two have become one—and they have achieved harmony with all that exists in the universe. Once again the problem of time is brought to our attention in Messiaen's own comments: "Time flows forgotten." They are "outside time" and not to be awakened.[65] Freed from time's tyranny, they have achieved liberty that has also released them from an authoritarianism antagonistic to love. One of the ways in which the tyranny of time is broken is through very subtle rhythmic patterns, as when the temple blocks play two rhythms: the first moving forward "towards ever longer durations . . . from the present towards the future; the other in a reverse [retrograde] direction, from very long towards less long durations, converting the future into the past."[66] The music of this movement, with elements operating both independently of each other and yet in a kind of apparently tenuous cooperation, is perceived as a wonderful and delicate *Klangfarbenmelodie*. The long, slow theme of love with the atonal bird songs and independent embroideries of clarinet, flute, and vibraphone, along with the rhythmic canon of the temple blocks, serves to conclude a movement characterized by orgiastic ecstasy.

Movement 7: "Turangalîla 2"

The apparently painful reaction that follows Movement 6, as if of the revenge of conscience, in "Turangalîla 2" may be compared to Song 3 ("Montagnes") in *Harawi*, in which the blackness of the abyss is encountered immediately following the beautiful expression of love in "Bonjour toi, colombe verte." As an expression of terror, however, some have found "Turangalîla 2" to be less than convincing. Drew feels that its melodies and rhythms "lack the breath of imaginative life which might have made the movement a worthy successor to the *Jardin du sommeil*."[67] However, the point being made seems to be that even here joy can be purchased only at the expense of some pain that will follow. Messiaen compared the mood of "Turangalîla 2" to Edgar Allan Poe's frightening short story "The Pit and the Pendulum." In this story, a prisoner of the Inquisition is placed in a darkened dungeon. Pacing around the dungeon's perimeters, he discovers a pit in which exist nameless horrors prepared for him if he should tumble into it. Later, the prisoner awakens to find himself tied up and is even more horrified to discover an inexorably descending pendulum from which is suspended a crescent-shaped scimitar poised to cut into his heart. Through quick thinking, he manages to have the rats gnaw away his bonds and hence to evade the blade. Only then does he notice that the walls of his dungeon are becoming hot and are closing in on him, and thus he has a choice between being roasted or falling into the pit:

> In an instant the apartment had shifted its form into that of a lozenge. But the alteration stopped not here—I neither hoped nor desired it to stop. I could have clasped the red walls to my bosom as a garment of eternal peace. "Death," I said, "any death but that of the pit!" Fool! might I have not known that *into the pit* it was the object of the burning iron to urge me? Could I resist its glow? or, if even that, could I withstand its pressure? And now, flatter and flatter grew the lozenge, with a rapidity that left me no time for contemplation. Its centre, and of course, its greatest width, came just over the yawning gulf. I shrank back—but the closing walls pressed me resistlessly onward. At length for my seared and writhing body there was no longer an inch of foothold on the firm floor of the prison. I struggled no more, but the agony of my soul found vent in one loud, long, and final scream of despair. I felt that I tottered upon the brink. . . . [68]

Even though the story ends with the rescue of the prisoner, not the happy ending but the fright and terror are the impressions that are left most indelibly on the reader's mind.

For such a crisis of the spirit, Messiaen chooses two musical devices that function as objective correlatives to express strongly felt emotion:

Turangalîla-symphonie   93

"a fan closing on itself," and a "terrifying rhythm," played by the percussion instruments.[69] The fan is created by the Ondes Martenot descending from above by means of half steps and the trombones ascending from below. The first two trombones ascend by chromatic seconds, while the third trombone and tuba ascend by intervals that create a kind of modulation by half-step from one tonal center to another. Messiaen has described the voice of the Ondes as "gentle, expressive . . . going down, full of pity, into the depths," while the trombones are compared to "monstrous dinosaurs,"[70] which must represent for him the primitive and bestial elements in man—something to be feared, and yet a necessary aspect of the human condition with which he must come to terms. The idea of such huge and frightening beasts in their unthinking movements about to destroy all before them, and in the end themselves becoming extinct, is terrifying. The "terrifying rhythm" is heard through fifteen measures of percussion sounds using triangle, woodblocks, bass drum, maracas, Turkish cymbal, and Chinese cymbal. Each instrument is paired with another: the triangle plays a pattern of sixteenth-note values, while the maracas retrogrades it; the woodblocks take their pattern forward, and the bass drum retrogrades it; finally the Turkish cymbal and the Chinese cymbal are paired in a pattern of forward and retrograde sixteenth notes.

Messiaen seems very exacting in his use of the words "pity" and "terrifying"; he must have been aware of Aristotle's dictum regarding the value of pity and terror or fear for true catharsis in tragedy. But *Turangalîla-symphonie* is ultimately not a tragedy but a carefully crafted work intended to say something about human experience that had not been previously expressed on this scale.

The piano solo begins the movement—a practice unusual even for Messiaen. Much of this solo has the reiterated high notes preceded by grace notes that we associate with bird songs, and eventually the *rāga-vardhana* rhythm appears. The section is closed by three cluster chords. The entire solo has been fast and *fortissimo* with brilliantly hammered sounds and is in strong contrast to the "fan" and the "terrifying rhythm," which have been previously noted. Following the latter, melodic interludes alternate with sections of the musical "fan," which returns with the intent of stimulating the same effect of fear and pity in the listener. The "fan," in this instance with the Ondes Martenot descending and the trombones ascending, and with the "melody of timbres" in both direct and retrograde forms, brings to a close the movement, which is capped by three cluster chords in the piano and a final terrifying drum beat.

Movement 8: Développement de l'amour"

Concerning the "terrible title" of this movement, "The Development of Love," the composer remarked that it is indicative of infinitely expanding passionateness like that of Tristan and Iseult, "who can never detach themselves," joined in love by the love potion. However, the title is also indicative of the musical structure. In such a long work, Messiaen said, a "few partial developments" could not serve: "there had to be a whole movement of development."[71]

Terror and pity are now almost left behind. These are now lovers who are never to be separated and whose love, "constantly growing," is "multiplying itself to the infinite." Their union thus is spiritual, and it is physical as well. As in the traditional Western marriage ceremony, the pair to be wed are proclaimed to become "one flesh," and so Friedrich Schlegel is said to have seen the goal of the entire human race to be "a progressive reintegration of the sexes."[72] And the Romantic writer Franz von Baader, who was influenced by Jakob Boehme, thought that the "true function" of sexual love involves helping "man and woman to integrate internally the complete human image, that is to say the divine and original image."[73] Messiaen similarly saw the expression and development of love as spiritual union that not only unites the lovers but also brings them into the realm of transcendence.

The use of the musical development is therefore symbolic, for both music and love are capable of being developed. But curiously, the musical development depends less on the conventional techniques of development than on a kind of flat repetition. Instead of fragmentation, inversion, retrogression, or modulation into foreign keys, Messiaen seems to have been content here to present the themes as they were heard in earlier movements. The familiar flower theme appears just as it was heard before, the statue theme is present in both original and canonic form, and the theme of love in two of its manifestations is prominent. The enchaining chords that were so much a part of the previous movements now have a new importance. Indeed, here Messiaen considered them to have thematic significance. Also present is soloistic material for piano alone, although here it is much truncated.

The structure of the movement is comprised of an introduction, consisting of a five-note motif of bell sounds juxtaposed with the chordal theme in the piano (Example 3.11). The motif in the bells is a linear form of the statue theme. The chords are Messiaen's superposed fourths, fifths, and seconds; there are four chords, used over and over in a litany effect,

Example 3.11

each of which can be analyzed as part of a different mode. The piano continues to expand on the chordal theme with ninth chords built on descending adjacent whole tones. There is a brief piano solo, marked near the close by a long, low trill, which leads to a passage dominated by the statue theme in the clarinets, bassoons, horns, trombones, and tubas.

Following the introduction begins the first development, which has the themes in the following order: chordal theme, theme of love as presented in the sixth movement, and the flower theme. The first development is made up of two appearances of the three themes plus the chordal theme, a central announcement of the theme of love using elements of its appearance in the second and fifth movements, and then two more appearances of the chordal, love, and flower theme series, completed by one more chordal section. The handling of the theme of love now elucidates its previous appearances and gives more evidence for the relatedness of the various instances of the theme. While at times it has seemed almost necessary to take the relatedness of the various manifestations of the theme on the basis of Messiaen's own testimony, here the intervallic relationships become clear. For example, the theme of love is directly related to its manifestation in the sixth movement (Example 3.12). The only differences between the two appearances involve those of key and instrumentation, the Ondes Martenot being omitted temporarily from the theme of love in the eighth movement.

The second development begins with what had been the central announcement of the theme of love in the first development. What marks this as a new section is the fact that the theme is now in the key of D major rather than in its previous key of C major. Following this announcement, nothing but chords and arpeggios are heard. No further

Example 3.12

use is made of either the flower theme or the theme of love until near the end of the second development, when the theme of love is heard. The chords and arpeggios are marked *avec passion, charnel et terrible*. This is another reminder that the pangs of conscience are still present and that passion, especially when it is manifested physically, is terrible and even terrifying.

Near the close of the second development, the theme of love appears for the last time. It also has been expanded to include more of the material from the sixth movement. Furious chords follow, and then the bells announce their five-note motif derived from the statue theme as heard at the beginning of the movement. The motif now reveals itself to be the first part of a three-part canon on the statue theme. The epilogue that closes the movement consists of the repetition of the brief piano solo heard earlier in the movement, a three-note motif from the original statue theme, and a decrescendo roll from the tam-tam and kettledrum. These last sounds in the movement, according to Messiaen, evoke "echoing vibrations in the caves of oracles . . . resonances from the languages of the beyond," while "the 'statue theme' bends over the abyss."[74] The "cave of oracles" seems reminiscent of the grotto in which Tristan and Iseult meet in the Tristan story and also of the grotto in which Pelléas and Mélisande meet in the Debussy-Maeterlinck opera. But Messiaen is not merely referring to a material cave, for he sees his music as linked to the "beyond," to transcendent meanings that connect *one to all that is*.

In order to achieve this level, however, it seems necessary to transcend the abyss of time.

When the terrifying "statue theme" looks down into the abyss, confronting a conscience beyond itself, a transcendental Time, and an unconscious replete with memories and feelings ordinarily avoided, the statue itself loses its menacing aspects. As in Messiaen's "Les Mains des Abîmes" in his *Livre d'Orgue*, the abyss can represent both human misery *and* the redemptiveness of divine grace. The terrifying statue theme has now been exorcized, and it does not return except in a transformed manner in the final movement to give the symphony a joyful closing.

Movement 9: "Turangalîla 3"

There is a return in "Turangalîla 3" to the formal qualities that have been encountered in "Turangalîla 1." Drew has remarked that, "if anything, the sounds are more glacial."[75] Nowhere does Messiaen explain the ideational content intended for this movement, which he described as "strange."[76] But since it follows the development of love, we are left to surmise that this movement continues to work out the fulfillment of the love that was consummated in the fifth movement. Further, since this movement is once again rich in formal devices, we may also see it as being linked with those movements in which ingenious thematic and rhythmic changes are being effected by the composer—in particular, the first, third, and seventh movements.

The luminescent tapestry of the theme here is highly complex but at the same time extremely lucid. The first or main portion of the theme outlines a descending major seventh, an ascending augmented fourth, an ascending major second, an ascending diminished fifth, a descending minor third, an ascending major second, and a descending ninth to an acciaccatura, which moves up to the closing note of the series by means of an ascending major second. The final tone of the series is, like the second, an E♭, a repetition that helps to give the theme a sense of direction and unity. Comparing this thematic material with the themes from "Turangalîla 1" and "Turangalîla 2," we find that only one interval—the descending major seventh—is identical, and that otherwise there are no similarities in intervallic relationships. But strangely the sounds of the themes from the first and third "Turangalîla" movements are not unlike. The contours of the themes in these two movements show their affinity for one another, and they move in each case through fairly wide dissonant intervals. Further, beyond mere thematic affinity is the feeling of

98   Olivier Messiaen and the Tristan Myth

calm and control; even when, in the latter part of "Turangalîla 3" the texture does get somewhat thicker, it never passes beyond the capacity of the ear to perceive individual instruments and melodic lines. The "fan" of "Turangalîla 2" and its differing texture, however, mark it as very unlike "Turangalîla 3."

Complex rhythmic schemes appear throughout "Turangalîla 3" and are carried out by woodblocks, suspended cymbal, maracas, Provençal cymbal, tam-tam, and bells.[77] As part of the luminescent design of the ninth movement, each of the five string parts is given its own *modus operandi*—that is, each is given one of Messiaen's modes of limited transposition. The first violins operate within Mode 3, the second violins within Mode 2, the violoncellos within Mode 4, and the contrabasses within Mode 1 (the whole-tone scale). In addition, each of the five string parts is paired with one of the rhythmic modes played by the five percussion instruments.[78] The overall effect, rather than of confusion, is clarity and extreme order.

Movement 10: "Final"

The formerly terrifying statue theme is at last fully transformed into a theme of joy. While a partial transformation had been presented in the fifth movement, now, in the final movement, the emotional content of the mythic structure and the musical form have been resolved: nothing remains but the "statue," without its menacing aspects, along with the overriding theme of love. Thus the one theme that pervades nearly the entire movement is the completely transformed statue theme. In its original manifestations the "statue" had been slow, ponderous, and loud; but like its fifth-movement transformation it is now fast, light, and yet fairly loud. The mood is brighter, and indeed seems turned upside down. Instead of plodding slowly from one low vertical third to a higher, traversing through a different key center for each third alighted on, the thirds now stay for a large part within the tonal center of F♯ major; furthermore, they encompass a small ambitus, and they proceed in the opposite direction from the earliest statue theme.

The structure of the movement is very clear, if slightly unconventional. It consists of two almost identical periods in which the theme is first presented in F♯ major, mainly outlining the tonic especially at its beginning and ending (Example 3.13). The statue theme appears thus twice, then it moves out to various keys. Another short period is inserted in which the theme is fragmented or developed by elimination. The ending

Example 3.13

Example 3.14

formula of the theme, with its three reiterated sixteenth notes, the last of which is tied to a dotted eighth note, is what is most noticeable (Example 3.14). In the recapitulation, the theme, played by the flutes, clarinets, and trumpets, stays in F# major, just as in a conventional recapitulation. Piano and strings double one another in parallel chords, ascending by whole and half steps. The Ondes Martenot and strings carry fragments of the theme, while other instruments punctuate the texture with sharp chords in F# major. There is a gigantic double "fan" created by the woodwinds and strings, first ascending and then descending, and at the same time the gamelan proceeds in the opposite direction, thus:

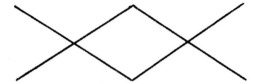

The fan leads into the most insistent presentation thus far of the theme of love, a variant of the one found in the sixth movement. The tremendous energy built up in the movement seems to have no possible ending, with its constant reiteration of transformed theme and fragmentations of that theme. Messiaen's solution to the near impasse is to have the Ondes Martenot cut through the musical tapestry of the leaping thematic material with two closing formulas. The first is short and outlines ascending tones both in and out of the key of F♯ major. The second outlines only tones in the tonic triad, ascending inexorably to A♯'''. This is followed by the long-held (five measures in all) tonic chord in F♯ that is the last sound heard in the symphony. The fermata and the marking *trés long* give some idea of the length Messiaen desired for this chord; these markings also reveal his conviction that this symphony, like the symphonies of Beethoven, must have an ending decisive and grand enough to bring such a massive work to a close effectively.

Turangalîla-symphonie is admittedly a gigantic work. Even though Gustav Mahler's Eighth Symphony exceeds it in length and in numbers of forces (adding vocal to instrumental), and even though Beethoven and Bruckner have exceeded its length in their ninth and eighth symphonies, respectively, Messiaen's great symphony nevertheless stands out as unusual for its duration and its ten-movement structure. It also is a work uniquely conceived in relation to a mythic armature, the Tristan story. Additionally, no other symphony stands at the center of a triptych in the way *Turangalîla-symphonie* embeds itself in Messiaen's Tristan trilogy.

The question of the structure of such a symphony as the *Turangalîla-symphonie* is inextricably tied to its meaning, especially since, as we have seen, it was Messiaen's intention to engage with the Tristan myth. But other material was also joined to his mythic armature—Ligeia, the Venus d'Ille, Breton's heroine in "L'Union Libre," and even Romeo and Juliet, in addition to the visual imagery from nature such as fruits, flowers, and birds. Each of these served to enrich and expand the essential structure. Themes are presented, modified, and transformed. Once the listener is apprised of the code he or she is able to make the associations the composer has invested in the material. But is there something intrinsic in

Turangalîla-symphonie 101

these themes that can express ideas such as terror in the statue theme, joy and pain in the theme of love, or the scent and color of flowers? For the elements that Messiaen was attempting to portray, he chose musical correlatives consistent with them. In the case of the terrifying "statue," he chose heavy trombones and a wide-ranging theme in thirds. We have noted the relationship of the theme with the "statue" of the Commendatore with its implications of doom in *Don Giovanni* and with the Coronation music for the guilt-ridden Boris in Mussorgsky's *Boris Godunov*. At other points where the feeling of terror is again desired by the composer, he chooses a "terrifying rhythm," which has a horrible uncertainty and an equally dreadful certainty within its pattern. For the flower theme, music of great delicacy is chosen, and for the theme of love both sweetness and torment are suggested by the constant weaving in and out of the tonal center by the high-pitched, insistent voice of the Ondes Martenot. Messiaen chose musical material out of which, always keeping in mind his mythic center, he effectively created a work that, as I have argued, is like an additive sculpture of gigantic proportions. The result is also identifiable as a structural analysis of the Tristan myth, which does for the twentieth century what Wagner's analysis of myth in music did for the nineteenth. *Turangalîla-symphonie* is a modern work that has affinities with such developments as Synthetic Cubism and Surrealism in art, but in a sense its value is predicated on its ability to reach back to ancient forms and mythic structures. The anthropologist Claude Lévi-Strauss has suggested that we listen to ourselves through music,[79] but more than this, Messiaen clearly intended *Turangalîla-symphonie* to be a reintegrative and transcendent experience for the listener.

NOTES

1. *Turangalîla-symphonie* was commissioned by Serge Koussevitzky and composed between July 1946 and November 1948; the first performance was by the Boston Symphony under Leonard Bernstein, with Yvonne Loriod as pianist, in December 1949. The score was published by Durand in 1953, and a revised score was issued in 1992. See *Olivier Messiaen: A Bibliographical Catalogue of Messiaen's Works* (Tutzing: Hans Schneider), 96–99, and Olivier Messiaen, *Music and Color: Conversations with Claude Samuel*, trans. E. Thomas Glasgow (Portland, Oregon: Amadeus Press, 1994), 156–57. Musical examples included in this chapter are from the revised edition © 1992 Éditions Durand; used by permission.

2. Olivier Messiaen, Program notes (trans. Paul Griffiths) accompanying *Turangalîla-Symphonie* (compact disk, Deutsche Grammophon 431 781–2), 4; this recording, made in 1990, is of the Opéra de Paris-Bastille orchestra under the direction of Myung-Whun Chung with Yvonne Loriod as pianist. Oddly, Mes-

102   Olivier Messiaen and the Tristan Myth

siaen elsewhere has said that he does not "believe in the 'concerto form'," which only great masters such as Mozart are capable of handling (Messiaen, *Music and Color*, 116–17). However, he has indicated that in Yvonne Loriod he found the perfect person to perform his works and that her capabilities at the keyboard helped him to shape his writing for the piano (Pierrette Mari, *Olivier Messiaen* [Paris: Seghers, 1965], 36; cf. Messiaen, *Music and Color*, 113).

3. Malcolm Hayes, "Instrumental, Orchestral and Choral Works to 1948," in *The Messiaen Companion*, ed. Peter Hill (London: Faber and Faber, 1994), 195.

4. Paul Griffiths, *Olivier Messiaen and the Music of Time* (Ithaca: Cornell University Press, 1985), 139.

5. Joanny Grosset, "Histoire de la musique: Inde," *Encyclopédie de la musique et Dictionnaire du Conservatoire*, ed. A. Lavignac (Paris: Delagrave, 1913–31), 1:1: 302. See also the discussion of the *Turangalîla-symphonie* in Robert Sherlaw Johnson, *Messiaen* (London: J. M. Dent, 1915), 82–94. In spite of Johnson's apology that his analysis of the work is "somewhat diffuse" (94), this book is nevertheless indispensable.

6. Messiaen, Program notes accompanying recording of *Turangalîla-Symphonie* (DGG 431 781–2), 1.

7. Ananda K. Coomaraswamy, *The Dance of Shiva*, revised ed. (New York: Noonday, 1957), 70–71.

8. A. L. Basham, *The Wonder That Was India* (1954; reprint New York: Grove Press, 1959), 322.

9. See S. M. Pandey and Norman Zide, "Surdas and His Krishna-*Bhakti*," in *Krishna: Myths, Rites, and Attitudes*, ed. Milton Singer (Honolulu: East-West Center Press, 1966), 177–78, 182–83, 187–88.

10. Ibid., 187.

11. Grosset, "Histoire de la musique: Inde," 303.

12. For the music accompanying this passage, see Richard Wagner, *Tristan und Isolde*, ed. Isolde Vetter, Sämtliche Werke 8, pts. 1–3 (Mainz: B. Schott's Sohne, 1990), 2:145–47.

13. Messiaen, Program notes accompanying recording of *Turangalîla-Symphonie* (DGG 431 781–2), 6.

14. See Walter S. Gibson, *Hieronymus Bosch* (New York: Praeger, 1973), 77–99.

15. Messiaen, Program notes accompanying recording of *Turangalîla-Symphonie* (DGG 431 781–2), 1–2.

16. See Eduard Hanslick, *Music Criticism 1846–99*, trans. Henry Pleasants (Baltimore: Penguin, 1963), 217.

17. In Wagner's version, the Morolt is Isolde's fiancé, while in the medieval sources he is her maternal uncle.

18. Italics added; for the music accompanying this passage, see Wagner, *Tristan und Isolde*, ed. Vetter, 3:4.

19. Messiaen, Program notes accompanying recording of *Turangalîla-Symphonie* (DGG 431 781–2), 2.

20. See Roger Sherman Loomis, *The Development of Arthurian Romance* (1963; reprint New York: W. W. Norton, 1970), 129–30.

21. Messiaen, Program notes accompanying *Turangalîla-Symphonie* (DGG 431 781–2), 8.

Turangalîla-symphonie   103

22. Prosper Mérimée, *The Venus of Ille and Other Stories*, trans. Jean Kimber (London: Oxford University Press, 1966), 29–30.

23. Ibid., 30.

24. Messiaen, Program notes accompanying recording of *Turangalîla-Symphonie* (DGG 431 781–2), 2.

25. See Messiaen, *Music and Color*, 178.

26. Messiaen, Program notes accompanying recording of *Turangalîla-Symphonie* (DGG 431 781–2), 2.

27. Ibid.

28. Ibid., 4.

29. Ibid., 2.

30. See Titus Burckhardt, *Alchemy*, trans. William Stoddart (Baltimore: Penguin, 1971), 139.

31. Ibid., 149.

32. Quoted in C. G. Jung, *The Psychology of Transference*, trans. R.F.C. Hull, Bollingen Series, 20 (Princeton: Princeton University Press, 1969), 85.

33. Leonard Burkat, "Current Chronicle," *Musical Quarterly* 36 (1950): 260.

34. Ibid.

35. Ibid.

36. Messiaen, *The Technique of My Musical Language*, trans. John Satterfield, 2 vols. (Paris: Alphonse Leduc, 1956), 1:67.

37. David Drew, "Messiaen—A Provisional Study (III)," *The Score and I.M.A. Magazine*, no. 14 (December 1955), 51.

38. Messiaen, *Music and Color*, 76.

39. For a modern edition, see *Les Maîtres musiciens de la renaissance française*, ed. Henry Expert (New York: Broude, n.d.), vols. 12–14.

40. Wilfrid Mellers, *François Couperin and the French Classical Tradition* (New York: Dover, 1968), 86.

41. Messiaen, Program notes accompanying recording of *Turangalîla-Symphonie* (DGG 431 781–2), 5.

42. Hayes, "Instrumental, Orchestral and Choral Works," 194.

43. Messiaen, Program notes accompanying recording of *Turangalîla-Symphonie* (DGG 431 781–2), 5.

44. Willi Apel, *Harvard Dictionary of Music*, 2nd ed. (Cambridge: Harvard University Press, 1969), 755.

45. Messiaen, *Music and Color*, 95.

46. Drew, "Messiaen—A Provisional Study [I]," *The Score and I.M.A. Magazine*, no. 10 (December 1954): 40.

47. Messiaen, Program notes accompanying recording of *Turangalîla-Symphonie* (DGG 431 781–2), 5.

48. Ibid., 2.

49. Werner Schmalenbach, *Chagall*, trans. M. Ledivelec (Milan: Uffizi Press, n.d.), 24.

50. Messiaen, Program notes accompanying recording of *Turangalîla-Symphonie* (DGG 431 781–2), 5. I have not been able to trace the alleged quotation attributed to Tristan in either the early sources or Wagner's music drama.

51. For the music accompanying these lines, see Wagner, *Tristan und Isolde*, ed. Vetter, 2:153.

52. Burckhardt, *Alchemy*, 149.

53. André Breton, *Poems*, ed. and trans. Jean-Pierre Cauvin and Mary Ann Caws (Austin: University of Texas Press, 1982), 48–51 (translation by permission of the translator).

54. Antoine Goléa, *Recontres avec Olivier Messiaen* (Paris: Julliard, 1960), 87.

55. Basham, *The Wonder That Was India*, 361–62, pl. LV (between 248–49).

56. Wilfrid Mellers, *Caliban Reborn* (London: Gollancz, 1968), 104.

57. Drew, "Messiaen—A Provisional Study (III)," 54.

58. Ibid.

59. Messiaen, Program notes accompanying recording of *Turangalîla-Symphonie* (DGG 431 781–2), 5.

60. Joseph Bédier, *The Romance of Tristan and Iseult*, trans. Hillaire Belloc (New York: Albert and Charles Boni, 1927), 71–72. At this point, Bédier claims to be relying on Béroul's early version of the story.

61. Gottfried von Strassburg, *Tristan*, trans. A. T. Hatto (Baltimore, Penguin, 1960), 272; Béroul, *The Romance of Tristan*, trans. Alan S. Fedrick (Baltimore: Penguin, 1970), 92–93, and, for the Old French text, see Béroul, *Le Roman de Tristan*, ed. Ernest Muret (Paris: Champion, 1967), ll. 2006ff.

62. Béroul, *The Romance of Tristan*, 92–93.

63. Messiaen, Program notes accompanying recording of *Turangalîla-Symphonie* (DGG 431 781–2), 6.

64. Ibid., 6.

65. Ibid.

66. Ibid., 5–6.

67. Drew, "Messiaen—A Provisional Study (III)," 55.

68. Edgar Allan Poe, *The Complete Works*, ed. James A. Harrison, 17 vols. (1902; reprint New York: AMS Press, 1965), 5:86.

69. Messiaen, Program notes accompanying recording of *Turangalîla-Symphonie* (DGG 431 781–2), 6.

70. Ibid.

71. Ibid.

72. Mircea Eliade, *The Two and the One*, trans. J. M. Cohen (New York: Harper and Row, 1965), 101, citing Friedrich Schlegel, *Über die Diotima*. Schlegel believed the end result of this process was to be the androgynous person.

73. Franz von Baader, *Sämmtliche Werke*, ed. Franz Hoffmann et al., 16 vols. (Leipzig: H. Bethmann, 1850–60), 3:309, as quoted in translation in Eliade, *The Two and the One*, 102.

74. Messiaen, Program notes accompanying recording of *Turangalîla-Symphonie* (DGG 431 781–2), 6.

75. Drew, "Messiaen—A Provisional Study (III)," 55.

76. Messiaen, Program notes accompanying recording of *Turangalîla-Symphonie* (DGG 431 781–2), 6.

77. For a description of the rhythm, see Audrey Ekdahl Davidson, "Olivier

Messiaen's Tristan Trilogy: Time and Transcendence" (Ph.D. diss., University of Minnesota, 1975), 267–69.

78. See also Burkat, "Current Chronicle," 266–67.

79. Claude Lévi-Strauss, *The Raw and the Cooked*, trans. John and Doreen Weightman (New York: Harper and Row, 1969), 17.

4

Cinq rechants: The Lovers Fly Away

Cinq rechants, the third and final part of Messiaen's Tristan trilogy, which the composer completed one month after finishing his symphony in 1948,[1] consists of five *rechants* or refrains for an unaccompanied chorus of twelve voices. The composition, which concludes the composer's work on the theme of love as experienced by Tristan and Iseult, is short in comparison with *Harawi* and *Turangalîla-symphonie*—approximately twenty minutes in length. The Tristan trilogy as a whole is like a Surrealist triptych in which the symphony is the central and largest panel, with unequal panels on each side. The function of the first panel, *Harawi*, is to introduce Messiaen's modern way of handling and analyzing the Tristan myth in music. The central panel is the broadest in its treatment of mythic and musical materials, but the final portion of the musical triptych is closely connected in theme and text to its other parts. As Robert Sherlaw Johnson comments, "A great deal of the material of *Cinq rechants* is derived from the subsidiary themes of *Turangalîla* and some from *Harawi*."[2] Using a text that is obscure and at times seemingly deliberately impenetrable, *Cinq rechants* combines fragmented language with musical texture and form that are extremely integrative. Nonsequential words and disjunct ideas hence find their place in the unifying

musical texture provided by the composer, who carefully blended together sounds and ideas in a final handling of an archetypal love story.

The structure that Messiaen adopted in *Cinq rechants* depends largely
on the Renaissance form found in Claude le Jeune's *chant-rechant* alternation in *La Printemps*, a collection of chansons published in 1603. The
musical texture of *Cinq rechants* is the most lucid of any of the three
works comprising the Tristan trilogy, with long passages of unison writing alternating with sections of two, three, four, or five-part harmony.
Only rarely does the texture expand to encompass eight, ten, or twelve
parts, which, since Messiaen specified a chorus consisting of twelve
voices, means that in a very few instances there will be one voice to a
part. Some spoken effects, such as the letters "t k t k" vocalized to create
percussive sounds and notated in a special diamond-shaped white notation, are also included. Messiaen's complex rhythmic patterns, including his use of Indian *talas* but also Greek meters, are present throughout.
Yet the overall effect is one of shimmering beauty.

If the form and texture are characterized by lucidity, the verse is another matter. Although the French words are, for the most part, in common parlance, the syntactic connections are often missing, and the style
is one of great disjunctiveness—and, therefore, of great mysteriousness.
Added to the opaque quality of the French text are segments of the
synthetic language that Messiaen forged from Sanskrit and Quechua syllables. "I composed *Cinq rechants*," he said, "on a poem written partly in
French, but mainly in a new language sometimes resembling Sanskrit
and sometimes Quechua."[3] This vocabulary—for example, "Cheu cheu
kapritama kalimolimo" in the third *rechant*—is not accessible to ordinary
rules of language. Concerning the freely invented language, Messiaen
explained that the words were selected because of their dynamics and
congruence with the rhythm of the music. The result, according to him,
involves easily combined dynamics, tone color, accents, and duration.[4]
Mellers has observed that these syllables dissolve " 'meaning' into purely
musical sound images," which "sometimes become bird or insect or animal noises."[5] Some of the sounds are rendered with the diamond-
shaped white notation.

For many, the difficulty in deciphering the composer's meaning in the
five poems that constitute his text for *Cinq rechants* is greater than the
effort of explicating the twelve poems of *Harawi*. The task of interpretation is also more complex here than with regard to the programmatic
design for *Turangalîla-symphonie*. It appears that Messiaen had, as Mari
suggests, "arrived at an impasse of the inexpressible."[6] In an interview

the composer had invoked Rainer Maria Rilke's *Duino Elegies* for the conception of love that is infinite and inaccessible to ordinary language.[7] For reasons of his own, then, the composer felt impelled to turn to a private language to express his deepest thoughts and feelings. As we have seen, he adopted the invented Sanskrit-Quechua language, and he revived the Surrealism that had informed his earlier poetry. However, the verse for *Cinq rechants* at times seems here to surpass Surrealism in certain aspects of its disjunctiveness and to approach the pastiche quality of Cubist painting and poetry.

Messiaen's debt to Surrealism has been noted in previous chapters. It is significant that the image of the lovers encapsulated in the crystal ball is derived from the work of the painter Hieronymus Bosch (see Figure 2), who is the Renaissance painter most admired by the Surrealists.[8] The first allusion to it comes in the "bulle de cristal" ("crystal bubble") of the first *rechant*,[9] where curiously the repetition in the music effectively imitates the claustrophobic smallness of the space in the bubble at the same time that an association is invoked with flight and stars—and hence, one would think, with freedom. But, paradoxically, toward the end of the text the stars are said to be stars of death. Also echoing through *Cinq rechants* are the designs of Marc Chagall, whose lovers in his paintings are transported by love.[10] Though Chagall was never a strict Surrealist, his work, like that of this school, dwells in the realm of fantasy and the dream world. So in *Cinq rechants* there is also the reconciliation of opposites or even impossibles; for example, one line contains the clashing images of "pieuvre de lumière" ("octopus of light"), wound, crowd, redden, and "ma caresse" ("my caress"). Here each term collides with the next without connectives. The composer's previously acknowledged admiration for André Breton seems relevant here; certainly, Breton's statement that "Beauty will be CONVULSIVE or will not be at all"[11] neatly characterizes the line from *Cinq rechants* cited here with its strange and arresting images.

As noted, another poet who seems to have influenced Messiaen's text is Pierre Reverdy, a reclusive mystic whose work is normally much less disjunctive than André Breton's poetry. Reverdy's poetry is more properly identified as Cubist because of the way it is assembled, often after the fashion of a collage or montage. Yet his texts in some instances are characterized by a lack of logical connections, and he has often been discussed as a writer of Surrealism.[12] At his most disjunctive he could create, for example, lines such as the following from "Auberge" ("Inn") evoked by an eye closing: "Au fond plaquée contre le mur la pensée qui ne sort pas" ("Deep inside and flat against the wall the thought which doesn't go out").[13] One may, of course, be reminded of the disjunctiveness that appeared in *Harawi*, especially in Song 9 in which the phrase "De l'eau, du temps, du ciel, l'escalier, du ciel" seems to have been simply dropped in elliptically and enigmatically. But almost every line of the verse in *Cinq rechants* is, like Reverdy's verse at its most disjunctive, characterized by ellipsis and enigma.

As in the earlier parts of the Tristan trilogy, major emphasis is placed on the love-death theme in the Tristan story. But Messiaen here took up material, including characters, not only from the love-death scene but also from other parts of the story. He specifically and prominently names Brangäne, the watchman of the *alba* or dawn song in Wagner's *Tristan und Isolde*. Isolde/Iseult herself, here apparently as in *Turangalîla-symphonie*, appears to be implicitly compared with the magician Vivian in the Arthurian legends, which to be sure are closely related to the Tristan story. Tristan seems to be the one meant in the reference to the "rameur d'amour" ("oarsman of love") in the fifth refrain; hence we are reminded that it was Tristan who was in charge of ferrying Iseult from Ireland to Cornwall, where she was to be King Mark's bride, and that it was during this voyage that they fell fatally in love. There is also another voyage that Iseult undergoes when she is drawn to what Messiaen called Tristan's "wondrous" crystal castle in Brittany.[14] And as we might expect, the love philter appears, curiously transformed in "philtres," all of which "sont bus ce soir" ("are drunk this night"). Finally there is the flower garden, which had appeared as a flowery bank in *Harawi* and as the "Garden of Love's Sleep" had formed the inspiration for the entire sixth movement of *Turangalîla-symphonie*. What is perhaps most important to note here is the way Messiaen stripped down all versions of the story to an even smaller ambitus of details, making his poetic rendition considerably more economical than the text of Wagner's music drama. Yet each individual part of the myth that Messiaen chose is absolutely essential, for together these parts form the mythic armature around which the music of *Cinq rechants* is structured.

At the same time that Messiaen in this composition had reduced the Tristan-Iseult myth to its bare essentials, he also enriched it in his syncretistic fashion through allusions and references to other mythological motifs and literary figures. Vivian had already been mentioned by Messiaen in his program notes for *Turangalîla-symphonie*, but now in the framework of *Cinq rechants* her importance for his understanding of life, love, and death is more fully revealed. Vivian, so called by Tennyson in his *Idylls of the King* but known as Nimue in Malory's *Morte d'Arthur*, learned Merlin's secrets by manipulating his love, and, becoming herself a magician, she turned the secrets against her master, whom she enclosed under a rock, in a cave, or in a hollow oak. She thus further becomes a part of the important network of imagery of enclosures and open spaces, and she also may be connected somehow with the magical powers possessed by Iseult, who has a miraculous ability to heal.

Other mythological or literary figures in the poetic imagery of *Cinq rechants* come from sources that are further afield. One is the ancient Greek, "l'explorateur Orphée" ("the explorer Orpheus"), who finds his heart in death in the first *rechant*, while another is Perseus, who slays the dread Medusa in the fifth *rechant*. Their stories are told in Ovid's *Metamorphoses*, but since their tales were familiar it is not necessary to seek a specific source for the composer's use of them. Indeed, at one time they were known to every schoolchild, though in bowdlerized versions. Orpheus, a "great symbol of love"[15] for Messiaen in *Cinq rechants*, would also have appealed to the composer on account of his role in Greek mythology as a musician with immense power. In a passage well known to music students, the medieval encyclopedist Isidore of Seville recounts the legend in which Mercury finds a tortoise shell with dried and stretched sinews; the messenger of the gods then passes this crude "lyre" on to Orpheus, who perfected its playing so that he was "deemed not merely to have swayed wild beasts with this art, but to have moved rocks and forests with the modulation of his song."[16] The beauty of his playing and singing also convinced the lord of the underworld to release his wife Eurydice to him to take back to the world of the living. Orpheus's descent into the abyss to rescue her and the power inherent in his music must have appealed to Messiaen. Eurydice was to follow Orpheus until *entirely* outside the lower world, and he was forbidden to look back. At the last moment, as he was leaving the precincts of the entrance to Hades, he fatally turned to her. Because she had not yet entirely stepped free from Hades, she was swallowed back into the underworld. This was an episode that Messiaen would have known intimately from a number of operas, including Christoph Willibald Gluck's *Orfée ed Euridice* or Claudio Monteverdi's *Orfeo*.[17] This story is not normally considered to be an analogue of the Tristan story, but, like the medieval hero, Orpheus too is an adventurer for love. The winding melodic line setting "l'explorateur Orphée trouve son coeur dans la mort" ("the explorer Orpheus finds his heart in death") may be described as paralleling his journey to the underworld, his tragic journey back to

112   Olivier Messiaen and the Tristan Myth

the upper world, and eventually, in some accounts, his reunion with Eurydice.

One must be more tentative, however, concerning Perseus, whose name merely appears linked with Medusa in a line that may seem at first to defy further analysis: "Persée Méduse l'abeille l'alphabet majeur" ("Perseus Medusa bee alphabet major"). But the Medusa story includes an episode of decapitation and hence may have been associated by the composer with the line "Coupe-moi la tête" ("Cut off my head") in Songs 5 and 9 of *Harawi* as well as in *Cinq rechants*. In the classical legend, Perseus's quest to kill the gorgon Medusa is successful, but when he finds that Polydeuctes has not kept his part of the bargain and has seduced Danäe after all, he unveils the fateful head of the gorgon, which turns the king to stone.[18] And yet one more dangerous character is introduced.

The first *rechant* makes mention of the villain Bluebeard, whose seventh wife, in Maurice Maeterlinck's drama, escapes from the prison of her husband's castle.[19] Messiaen's text specifically calls attention to the seventh door through which escape is made: "Barbe Bleu(e) château de la septième porte" ("Bluebeard castle of the seventh door"), sung by the basses and alternating here with the pseudo-Quechua words, variously "Ha kapritama," "Hayo kapritama," and "Hayoma kapritama." Maeterlinck's play would have been known to Messiaen through Paul Dukas's operatic version, *Ariane et Barbe Bleu*,[20] in which the heroine's name contains a hint of that Ariadne who solved the riddle of the Minotaur's labyrinth, thus saving her lover, Theseus, who later deserted her. Rollo Meyers comments:

> In the libretto, written specially for Dukas by Maeterlinck (whose *Pelléas et Mélisande* had already been set by Debussy), a new variant of the well-known Blue-Beard legend is proposed whereby Ariane persuades Blue-Beard to allow her to offer the other captive wives their freedom. And when they are too timid to accept it, preferring the captivity they know to a liberty of which they are afraid, Blue-Beard does nothing to prevent Ariane herself from leaving the Castle and returning to the light of day.[21]

Concerning Dukas's version of the story, Gustave Samazeuilh has commented: "The character of Ariane symbolizes the liberating pity which struggles against the enslavement and feebleness of humanity, and endeavours to educate toward a higher consciousness those souls which are not yet sufficiently developed to understand its significance."[22] The door mentioned by Messiaen in *Cinq rechants* is a door of freedom. In *Harawi*, the *bien aimée* had been the liberating force; in *Turangalîla-symphonie*, the great feminine magicians—Vivian, Ligeia, and Iseult—were acclaimed. Now, in *Cinq rechants*, Ariane from Maeterlinck's play, as another of these magical characters though her name is not spoken, thus adds another layer to our understanding of the figure of Iseult. These allusions make reference to love, death, entrapment, and rescue—themes that are continued from *Harawi* and *Turangalîla-symphonie*.

However, the text of *Cinq rechants* contains yet further imagery that is not easily identifiable in relation to source or theme. For example, in the second *rechant* there are the four lizards. These obscure creatures, however, may involve an allusion to the Bosch triptych, in particular the left panel, "Earthly Paradise," which contains depictions of lizards (Figure 2). Another possible source of inspiration for the image might have come from the Surrealist René Char's poem "Complainte du lézard amoureux," in which the lizard is enamored of a goldfinch, which is sitting vulnerably on a sunflower; this poem was set to music by Messiaen's former student, Pierre Boulez, in the same year in which *Cinq rechants* was written.[23] The line of text, with its reference also to the flute and to rocking, and the music, in which the melody rocks back and forth on tritones, do seem to signify tenderness. The lizards return in the fifth and final *rechant*. Then in the third *rechant* there is the curious "pieuvre de lumière" ("octopus of light"), or the octopus with "tentacles d'or" ("golden tentacles") in the fifth *rechant*. But these also could possibly have been inspired by the same painting by Bosch, who painted a strange fruitlike creature with ivory-gold tentacles in the central panel. This octopuslike creature in the painting is pulling into itself a group of people, perhaps lovers, and swallowing them. Additionally, in Roland Penrose's painting *The Invisible Isle* (Figure 1), important to Messiaen since it provided one element of inspiration for Song 9 of *Harawi*, the hair of the woman, who is suspended between earth and heaven, resembles golden tentacles, which envelop the tiny island. It is possible that this painting may also have been important to the composer in providing inspiration for "Pieuvre aux tentacles d'or" in the final *rechant*.

Like the earlier parts of the Tristan trilogy, *Cinq rechants* retains Messiaen's obsession with the matter of time. Perhaps even more than previously he emphasizes the idea that time can be transcended. Messiaen commented that, despite the rhythmic symbolism suggesting life's briefness, the loved one stands "above Time, beyond any musical rhythmical or literary technique, even beyond death"—a condition, in his view, comparable to Poe's Ligeia.[24] For the lovers, time is transcended and yet is accessible to them in all of its forms—past, present, and future. As the text for the fourth *rechant* unsyntactically states, "Tes yeux voyagent, dans le passé" ("your eyes voyaging, in the past").

But in this final composition in the trilogy even more pervasive than the theme of time is the theme of space, since the very first words in the French text of the first *rechant* are "Les amoreaux s'envolent, Brangien dans l'espace tu souffles" ("The lovers fly off, Brangäne, you breathe into space"). The levitating lovers signify that the love of Tristan and Iseult is so expansive that it stretches beyond the bounds of the earth. Other images of space within the text of *Cinq rechants* include enclosures such as "corbeille courbe" ("curved plot of flowers"), "ma prison d'amour" ("my prison of love"), "cercle du jour" ("circle of day"), the grotto, castle, and, perhaps most significant of all, the crystal bubble in which the lovers are enclosed as in Bosch's triptych (Figure 2). But the spaces of enclosure are neatly balanced against images of expansion, thus suggesting the observation that though there is a limiting aspect to love (after all, it confines one within a tighter relationship than mere friendship), its expansive potentialities are also inherent in a love relationship.

Messiaen's paradoxical insistence on the images of openness and expansiveness, and at the same time of enclosed space, hiddenness, and even claustrophobia, governs each of the five poems set to music in *Cinq rechants* to a surprising extent. In the first poem, then, the lovers fly off into space; also present is Bluebeard's seventh door, which entails some risk in opening but produces rewards as well. In the second poem, the fan is both closed and unfolded and hence, though here appearing to be associated with birdsong and joy, is reminiscent of the musical "fan" from *Turangalîla-symphonie* and its associations of terror derived from Poe's "The Pit and the Pendulum." The third poem depicts not only a prison of love, but also a new expansive landscape as well. In the fourth, the bouquet is undone, loosened, but there are rose-colored shutters, which can enclose. Finally, in the last poem of *Cinq rechants*, extended arms, an image of openness, are juxtaposed with the enclosed garden.

The polarities of the images of openness and enclosure of the kind used in *Cinq rechants* have received perceptive treatment in Gaston Bachelard's *Poetics of Space*. Bachelard's phenomenological study first deals with openness and the feeling of exaltation and immensity that is often common to the poetic experience. He quotes a saying that he attributes to Rilke—"The world is large, but in us it is as deep as the sea"[25]—which perhaps involves a perception that Messiaen himself was attempting to describe in his quotation of Juliet's words: "My bounty is as boundless as the sea." For the novelist, poet, and philosopher O. V. de L. Milosz, whom Bachelard also cites, the "exaltation of space goes beyond all frontiers. 'Away with boundaries, those enemies of horizons! Let genuine distance appear!' And further: 'Everything was bathed in light, gentleness and wisdom; in the unreal air, distance beckoned to distance. My love enveloped the universe'."[26] The expansiveness of love for Messiaen leads to a freedom previously achieved only in part of Song 11 ("Katchikatchi les étoiles") of *Harawi* and in the fifth and tenth movements of *Turangalîla-symphonie*. There are still elements that are found to be distressing in *Cinq rechants*, but these are now subordinated to the safety of enclosures, and, even beyond that, to the freedom of flying away into space.

The musical material with which Messiaen chose to enwrap his mythic center—that is, the Tristan story—again has many sources. His principal source with regard to musical structure was revealed in the program notes for the sound recording of *Cinq rechants* that he supervised: Claude le Jeune's *Le Printemps*.[27] As indicated previously, this collection of Le Jeune's *chansons* contains pieces made up of alternating *rechants* (refrains having a recurring text and music) and *chants* (couplets having a new text, a varying texture, and a different melody from the refrain—but a melody basically similar to every other recurrence of the *chant* within that song form). Messiaen's adaptations of the form are varied from section to section. In the first *rechant*, he included an introduction, refrain, couplet, refrain, couplet, refrain, and coda, while, for example, the third, which, as Mellers suggests, forms "an apex to the whole work,"[28] contains introduction, couplet, refrain, couplet, refrain, couplet, and coda. The refrain and couplet form, which Messiaen had used in the second movement of *Turangalîla-symphonie*, was influenced also by the design of the medieval rondeau with its repeated refrain.

Messiaen's indebtedness to medieval form is supported not only by the line "Troubadour Viviane Yseult" but also by his actual acknowledgment of influences from medieval song. Specifically, he named the songs of the troubadours Jaufre Rudel, Folquet de Marselha, and Guiraut de Bornelh, whose "Reis glorios" is the most famous of the *albas* or dawn songs.[29] It is apparent that attitudes and emotions expressed in the text of "Reis glorios" as well as in Jaufre's "Lanquan li journ son lonc en may"[30] and Folquet's "Vers Dieu"[31] give us insight into Messiaen's entire trilogy. In "Reis glorios," which has also been mentioned here in connection with *Harawi*, the troubadour begins with a pious salutation to God, but soon launches into his prayers for and his worries about the companion who has been attending a lady (presumably another knight's wife) "since the night came on." As Peter Dronke notes, "After [the] resplendent opening, the watcher continues in less exalted tones, waking his friend, warning him of danger, cajoling him to rise; he claims to have been on his knees praying for the lover's safety all night."[32] Folquet's "Vers Dieu" contains some of the same pious exclamations, but addressed to the Blessed Virgin. The song seems to be a completely innocent one, since it praises St. Mary, her Son, God the Father, and the Holy Spirit without mentioning anything clandestine. However, the style of Folquet's song is the same as that of secular troubadour song. As Jonathan Saville implies, the line between the pious song and the "God-help-my-friend-to-commit-adultery" song is a very thin one.[33] There is no doubt, however, about the meaning behind Jaufre's love song "Lanquan li journ son lonc en may." In this song, the poet frankly admits that he burns for his far-away loved one.[34] This song, identified by one critic as "the greatest achievement of Jaufre,"[35] interestingly mentions the lady's own room and her garden space; thus we see once again how pervasive are the metaphors of enclosure, particularly of the garden, in medieval poetry. Hence we also see how Messiaen was truly heir to the troubadour-trouvère tradition, for his own reforging of the medieval Tristan myth *consciously* drew on the very same categories of experience and imagery that were opened up by the medieval poets of Provence and France.[36]

Direct musical parallels between troubadour songs and Messiaen's practice, however, would be harder to prove, since his melodies so often exploit dissonant intervals such as the tritone and usually have a wider range than the medieval melodies with their comfortable vocal range. Perhaps a certain melodic or rhythmic suppleness found in some linear portions of the couplets may be related to the melodies and rhythms found in more free transcriptions of medieval song. Also, each separate phrase of troubadour-trouvère song is attached neatly to the next, much as one piece of a mosaic fits into the space next to another; thus Messiaen's additive method of linking phrases to one another seems congruent with the medieval song writer's equally additive and cumulative method.

Messiaen also claimed that the Peruvian *yaravi* or *harawi*, which he had drawn upon for his song cycle *Harawi*, provided him with one of the sources for his melodic inspiration in *Cinq rechants*.[37] However, here he

Cinq rechants 117

abandoned the very frank way in which he had taken over the Peruvian melodies for the first part of the trilogy with actual tunes being borrowed and transformed by the composer. It is indeed impossible to show a direct connection between the melodies of these five *rechants* and the songs found in the collection, edited by the d'Harcourts, which Messiaen had used as his source of Peruvian melody. In contrast with *Harawi*, which contains specific Quechua melodies that had been passed through Messiaen's deforming compositional prism, no direct relationship with the music of any Peruvian song may be discovered in *Cinq rechants*. What *Harawi* and *Cinq rechants* have in common, in addition to the mythic core of the Tristan myth, is Messiaen's musical language, which utilizes the ascending and descending tritone; chromaticisms; wide, dissonant leaps, and the added nonretrogradable rhythms.

"RECHANT 1"

The five *rechants* of *Cinq rechants* trace moods and themes and, in so doing, add new layers to our understanding of myth and music and their interaction. The text of the first *rechant* may be translated as follows:

Introduction	Hayo kapritama, la li la li la li la ssaréno.
Refrain 1	The lovers fly off, Brangäne, you breathe into space,
	The lovers fly off, toward the stars of death.
	t k t k t k t k
	[Furious laughter] ha ha ha ha ha thirst
	The explorer Orpheus finds his heart in death.
Couplet 1	Star mirror star castle Iseult, from love separated.
	Hayoma kapritama
	Starry crystal bubble my return.
	Hayoma kapritama
Refrain 2	The lovers fly off, Brangäne, you breathe into space.
	The lovers fly off, toward the stars of death.
	t k t k t k t k
	[Furious laughter] ha ha ha ha ha
	The explorer Orpheus finds his heart in death.

Couplet 2	Star mirror star castle Iseult, from love separated.
	Starry crystal bubble my return.
	Bluebeard castle of the seventh door
	Hayoma kapritama
	t k t k t k t k
Refrain 3	The lovers fly off, Brangäne, you breathe into space.
	The lovers fly off, toward the stars of death.
	t k t k t k t k
	[Furious laughter] ha ha ha ha ha thirst
	The explorer Orpheus finds his heart in death.
Coda	Hayo kapritama, la li la li la li la ssaréno.

Messiaen begins with the freedom of space, the prison of enclosed space, separation, and death. Yet, in spite of the three "darker" themes, there appears to be no real feeling of tragedy projected by the first *rechant*, since the theme of freedom of space is reiterated near the close, in the third refrain, and thus seems to establish the prevailing tone of the piece. Hence whatever dark and threatening elements are present, these seem to be neatly balanced by the more joyful elements.

In the first couplet, the initial theme that sets the words concerning the "miroir étoile" ("star mirror"), "château d'étoile" ("star castle"),[38] and the "bulle de cristal" ("crystal bubble") are as shimmeringly translucent as the words they set. There are here essentially two melodic themes in the soprano line. The first theme, which sets the text dealing with the enclosure of the crystal castle and with Iseult's separation from love, is itself a circular one, since it is made up of only four tones used again and again. The melody rocks back and forth on the descending tritonal intervals from d♮" to a♭ and the diminished fourth from e♭" to b♮'. The melody finally breaks out of its repetitiveness with two additional tones, d♮' and f♮', which bring the phrase to a close. Messiaen claimed that he used *tala miçra varna* in this part of the couplet,[39] but the *tala* is not used in its totality nor is it used consistently. The portion of the *miçra varna* that he used consists of the first four values:

The fragmentary form of the *tala* appears at the words "Yseult d'amour," with note values doubled (Example 4.1).

Example 4.1

Messiaen's text for the soprano line then treats the crystal bubble as in Bosch's painting (Figure 2). The obstinate repetition of c♯" imitates the smallness of the space within the bubble, then the melodic line moves up by means of the interval of a tritone to a g♮"—a leap upward that constitutes a strange kind of "escape" at the point where there should be a "retour" or return. Strict word painting, however, had never been a goal for Messiaen. At the same time, the contralto line, consisting of reiterated words in Messiaen's invented language, also falls into two phrases, but because of the difference in length of the phrases in the two voices, the point at which they meet will be constantly shifting, with new intervallic relationships created at each measure.

"RECHANT 2"

The balance of enclosure and freedom appears again in the second *rechant*, as implied in its first couplet in which the fan is both unfolded and closed:

> Couplet 1   My first time earth earth the fan unfolded
> My latest time earth earth the fan closed
> Luminous my laughter of shadow my young star
> on the streams.
> Ah
> Flute solo, rock the four lizards as you depart.

The fan is an effect that is duplicated in the music. The words "ma première fois terre terre l'éventail déployé" ("My first time earth earth the fan unfolded") are set to a melody that is made up of only five tones. The melody rises and falls, like a fan opening and closing, and teases the ear with its alternation of perfect fourths with tritones. When in the same couplet the first soprano sings the words "lumineux mon rire d'ombre" ("luminous my laughter of shadow"), she is joined by the unison chorus at "ma jeune étoile sur les fleuves" ("my young star on the streams"). The melody here is based on tones that are very nearly chromatic. The phrase rises, then vacillates, and finally falls by means to the tritone and comes to rest on a repeated c♮'. The rhythmic meters are precisely notated and resemble portions of the *talas* known as *nihçankalîla* and *turangalîla*.[40]

The text continues:

Refrain 1   Mayoma kapritama ssarimâ

Couplet 2   My first time earth earth the fan unfolded
My latest time earth earth the fan closed
Luminous my laughter of shadow my young star
on the streams.
Ah
Flute solo, rock the four lizards as you depart.
Mano mano mano nadja lâma krîta makrîta mayo
ma yo ma
Ma yo ma yo mata krî mata krîma lâda na noma
noma

Refrain 2   Mayoma kapritama ssarimâ

Coda   Mano mano nadja lâma krîta
Ma yo ma yo mata krî
Flute solo, rock the four lizards as you depart.

In the second couplet, as in the first, both "laughter" and "shadow" are present, while the beauty of a flute solo is juxtaposed with the reptilian creatures, the lizards, which have been noted previously. The effects throughout are very subtle. Not implausibly Messiaen might have been thinking of Debussy's virtual flute solo with orchestral accompaniment in *The Afternoon of a Faun*,[41] which, inspired by Mallarmé's poem about a faun that has an erotic dream, may throw light on the lizards, faunlike in their sensuality, in *Cinq rechants*. At the end of the *rechant* the coda slows to a *rallentando molto* and fades away to a near whisper.

"RECHANT 3"

The philter with its associations with love and death is the controlling image in the third *rechant*:

Cinq rechants

Introduction	My gown of love my love
	My prison of love made of light air.
	Lîla, lîla, my memory, my caress.
	Mayoma ssari ssari man(e) thikâri
Couplet 1	Oumi annôla oumi oumi annôla oumi sarî sarîsa
	Cheu cheu mayoma kapritama kalimolimo
	flouti yoma
	Trianguillo tender gown
	All the beauty, landscape new
Refrain 1	Troubadour Vivian Iseult, all the circles all the eyes.
	Octopus of light wounds, crowds, rose-colored my caress
Couplet 2	Oumi annôla oumi oumi annôla oumi sarî sarîsa
	Cheu cheu mayoma kalimolimo cheu
	flouti yoma
	Trianguillo tender gown
	All the beauty, landscape new
Refrain 2	Troubadour Vivian Iseult, all the circles all the eyes.
	Octopus of light wounds, crowds, rose-colored my caress
Couplet 3	Oumi annôla oumi oumi annôla oumi sarî sarîsa
	flouti yoma
	Cheu cheu mayoma kalimolimo kalimolimo
	flouti yoma
	[Very loud] Ha
Coda	All the philters are quaffed again tonight.
	[Caressingly] Ha

There is also the reiteration of entrapment, enclosure, as in "Ma robe d'amour" ("My gown of love"), or even claustrophobia in the second reference to the Bosch painting (see Figure 2): "Ma prison d'amour faite d'air léger" ("My prison of love made of light air"). The enigmatic reference to the octopus is also found in the first refrain in this *rechant*, which likewise includes the line that links the troubadours, Vivian, and Iseult "tous les cercles tous les yeux" ("all the circles, all the eyes"). The latter phrase is congruous with the circular, encircling images in all of the five poems of Cinq *rechants*. Here eyes are appropriately connected

122   Olivier Messiaen and the Tristan Myth

with circles, for by the act of *seeing* men and women are caught up in love, which for Messiaen was in part symbolized by the enclosed space of the circle, as we have seen. Separate themes set the line "Troubadour Viviane Yseult tous les cercles tous les yeux" and the invoking of the octopus. The first has a rhythmic structure resembling the *tala hamsalîla*.[42]

In this *rechant* the third couplet receives an exceedingly elaborate treatment in comparison with the two couplets that have come earlier. Its first section is built according to a mathematically precise plan of overlapping. Pairs of chords move adjacently by parallel and contrary motion with the series not moving always onward and upward but retrogressing to an earlier pair of chords and then proceeding from that point. The chords are virtually unsingable except by persons with absolute pitch, since they are composed of extremely thick clusters of major and minor seconds in combination with thirds, fourths, and an occasional fifth. This section begins *piano* and crescendos into the second interpolated section, which consists of a repeated cascading melodic phrase on the syllable "Ha," signifying laughter. This phrase is the basis for a twelve-part "canon." The melodic material is treated in the following manner: There are two descending minor seconds, a descending perfect fourth, another descending minor second, and one more descending perfect fourth; the melody then rises a major seventh, descends a major seventh, repeats the same rising major seventh, and then falls the distance of a diminished fifth. Each of the twelve voices retains the same intervallic relationships for its own phrase, except that each one, entering at the delay of an eighth note value, begins a whole tone lower than the last. The first soprano repeats the melodic pattern five full times, with each of the lower voices entering later and being able to complete only some portion of the five entrances. The chords on "yoma," unlike the previous appearance of these chords, now include ten of the voices, while the other two, the second and third tenors, speak the word "sarî" in regular sixteenth-note values. This section begins *fortissimo* and ends *forte fortissimo*, with a pause of three and one-half beats separating it from the coda that follows—a coda that concludes with a soprano solo, *piano, souple et caressant*, accompanied by the other voices softly humming. The soloist sings "Ha," a syllable that, when sung loudly and boisterously, sounds like derisive laughter. Here it sounds like a sigh—"Ah."

"RECHANT 4"

In contrast to the spatial imagery of enclosure and expansion in the previous *rechant*, Messiaen's text for the fourth *rechant* presents a tension

Cinq rechants   123

in its display of light-dark imagery, as in "amour du claire au sombre" ("love from light to dark"). But more obviously it makes particular use of nonsignifying words in his synthetic language, repeated and embedding a scanty French text.

Refrain 1	Niokamâ palalan(e) souki My bouquet all undone is radiant Niokhamâ palalan(e) soukî The rose-colored shutters Oha, love, love, from light to dark Oha
Couplet 1	Roma tama tama tama ssouka rava kâli vâli ssouka ssouka nahame kassou
Refrain 2	Niokhamâ palalan(e) soukî My bouquet all undone is radiant Niokhamâ palalan(e) soukî The rose-colored shutters Oha, love, love, from light to dark Oha
Couplet 2	Roma tama tama tama ssouka rava kâli vâli ssouka naham(e) kassou
Refrain 3	Niokhamâ palalan(e) soukî My bouquet all undone is radiant Niokhamâ palalan(e) soukî The rose-colored shutters Oha, love, love, from light to dark Oha
Couplet 3	Roma tama ssouka rava kâli vâli ssouka nahame kassou
Refrain 4	Niokhamâ palalan(e) soukî My bouquet all undone is radiant Niokhamâ palalan(e) soukî The rose-colored shutters Oha, love, love, from light to dark Oha
Coda	Roma tama my bouquet is radiant [Supple] Ah my bouquet is radiant.

In the first refrain, the text describes "Mon bouquet tout défait rayonne" ("My bouquet all undone is radiant"), which suggests the disintegration brought about by love before reintegration can take place, but the musical material here is highly integrated and severely limited. All the voices are used in unison. The meters are constantly changing and include a portion of *tala miçra varna*[43] which differs slightly from the portion used in the first *rechant*. The following couplet is to be performed in a monotone, according to the instructions in the score, and uses only the text "Roma tama ssouka rava kâli vâli ssouka nahame kassou," set to an extremely limited melodic ostinato at the beginning of the phrase but branching out into new material at the words "ssouka rava kâli vâli."

Throughout the remainder of the *rechant* a very small amount of melodic material—material dominated by the tritone with a narrow accompaniment consisting of tritonal intervals varied by some rhythmic changes—is economically utilized. There is no sign that the composer's invention was flagging, for this *rechant* seems deliberately to move closer to the form used by Claude le Jeune which consisted of similar or even identical refrains and couplets. In the concluding coda the laughter ("Ha") is performed by a single soprano with all the other voices joining at the final "Ha mon bouquet rayonne" ("Ah my bouquet is radiant").

"RECHANT 5"

The concluding *rechant* knits together all the strands of love-death, enclosure-freedom, flower, melody, octopus, and lizard; the text is translated thus:

Introduction	Mayoma kalimolimo mayoma kalimolimo
	Your eyes voyaging in the past
	Solar melody of curved flower garden
	t k t k t k t k
Couplet 1	Diamond-shaped my flower forever
	Flako flako
	Philter Iseult oarsman of love
	Flako flako
	Fairy Vivian to my song of love
	circle of day.
	Hayo tramples, reddens hayo arms extended
	Octopus with tentacles of gold
	Perseus Medusa bee alphabet major.

Refrain 1	Droning flower turns toward death,
	Four lizards the grotto octopus and death:
	[Furiously] Corolla which bites second makes sure
	it eats first.
	Ha.
Reprise of	Droning flower turns toward death.
Refrain	Four lizards the grotto octopus and death:
	[Furiously] Corolla which bites second makes sure
	it eats first.
	Ha
Couplet 2	Diamond-shaped my flower forever
	Flako flako
	Philter Iseult oarsman of love
	Flako flako
	Fairy Vivian to my song of love
	circle of day.
	Hayo tramples, reddens hayo arms extended
	Octopus with tentacles of gold
	Perseus Medusa bee alphabet major.
	t k t k t k t k
Coda	[Vigorously] Mayoma kalimolimo mayoma kalimo-
	lino
	t k t k t k t k
	in the future
	[Very softly] um

The second couplet of this *rechant* introduces Medusa, the terrible feminine figure whose snake-covered head was cut off by Perseus; hence we are reminded of Songs 5 ("L'amour de Piroutcha") and 11 ("Katchikatchi les étoiles") of *Harawi* and the tortured cry "Cut off my head!" Now the threatening seat of sensibility is removed, and all the terrifying images of the two previous works in the Tristan trilogy as well as of the present work are laid to rest.

The introduction to the *rechant* begins with the pseudo-Quechua words "Mayoma kalimolimo" and continues with "Tes yeux voyagent, dans le passé" ("Your eyes voyaging in the past") and "Mélodie solaire de corbeille courbe" ("Solar melody of curved flower garden"). Past, present, and future are not separate entities; like Hénri Bergson, Messiaen thought of all as being present simultaneously and being equally acces-

Example 4.2

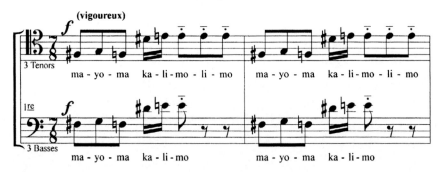

sible. Time and space also are integrated here, since the eyes travel in the past just as in the first poem of *Cinq rechants* the lovers traveled into space. So Tristan must be the voyager, an "oarsman of love" ("rameur d'amour"), as he and Iseult journey to Cornwall, which is King Mark's land. But there is also journeying into the past to bring us to the fairy Vivian of Arthurian legend. And there is the further journeying into time, into antiquity and Greek legend, which reports the story of Perseus's beheading of Medusa—all of which is brought into the present through the mnemonic function of the verse. There is additionally in the introduction a linking of solar melody and the curved flower garden.

"Mélodie solaire" may confidently be interpreted as Messiaen's recognition of the ancient idea of the harmony of the spheres in which the cosmos is fully in tune, with the planets making harmonious sounds as they turn about the earth. Thus a diagram in Robert Fludd's *Utriusque Cosmi Historia* (1617) shows the sun and the other planets each tuning to its own particular note.[44] The idea was set forth by the ancients, but was discredited from a scientific point of view when the Ptolemaic universe was superseded by Copernicus's heliocentrism. But for Messiaen the idea of a "solar melody" was not frivolous, for he understood it in his Tristan trilogy as relating to the way in which the experience of love perfects one and brings the person into tune with the cosmos.

Four themes set the text of the introduction, beginning with a setting of the words "Mayoma kalimolimo" in vigorous 7/8 meter and sung in unison by the tenors and basses (Example 4.2). The second theme sets "Tes yeux voyagent" for unison sopranos and contraltos (Example 4.3). "Dans le passé" ("in the past") has three repeated quarter notes, followed by a tritone in the form of doubled vertical intervals, sung by contraltos and basses. The tritone appears on the last syllable (Example 4.4). Then

Example 4.3

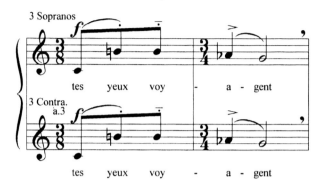

Example 4.4

the supple melody that sets the text "Mélodie solaire de corbeille courbe" ("solar melody of curved flower garden") appears as an unaccompanied soprano solo. This melody is both heavily chromatic and tritonal, and is almost completely within the whole-tone scale and utilizes fairly regular rhythms (Example 4.5).

The garden here is clearly a garden of love, which is to be imagined filled with plants, flowers, and brightly colored songbirds. Its curvature is a reminder of the perfection inherent in the shape of the circle. A section of the spoken sounds "t k t k" follows the "solar melody" passage, and the introduction closes with a repetition of the music that previously had set "dans le passé," but this time on the closed-mouth syllable "um." Then the *rechant* moves on to the first couplet.

After the second couplet, the concluding coda repeats the "mayoma kalimolimo" section of the introduction, but omits the "Tes yeux voyagent" and "Mélodie solaire" sections. There is once again a passage of "t k t k"—sounds that are reminiscent of the monkey chant in *Harawi*.

Example 4.5

The coda ends with the words "dans l'avenir," set to the repeated tones and the tritone interval that had been used to set "dans la passé" in the introduction. Here the future has the last word. The story of the lovers does not end, but goes on into time that has not yet been actualized but that must necessarily come into being on account of the laws of temporality. As Mellers notes, "the same neutral tritone symbolizes the before and the after, of which we can have no certain knowledge."[45]

In *Cinq rechants*, the musical material seems to come under tighter control and at the same time to be more economical than in either *Harawi* or *Turangalîla-symphonie*. The control and the economies are evidenced in the texture, which is thinner than in either of the earlier works in the trilogy (large sections are completely monodic or unisonal), and they are also shown in the persistent use of the tritone, which appears in virtually every important melodic theme in the work. Tighter control might also be seen in Messiaen's consistent use of Indian rhythmic patterns and his notation of these rhythms in a precise metrical system, which accounts for each sixteenth-note value, instead of considering them to be added values in irrational measures, as was done, for example, in *Harawi*. At the same time that these rhythmic values are more precisely notated, the inevitable wrench caused by the odd number of beats leads the listener away from regular "square" Western rhythms and a Western sense of time. The control and economy are especially seen in the fourth *rechant*, which is overwhelmingly tritonal both harmonically and melodically.

The influence of Claude le Jeune's *Le Printemps* means that Messiaen, like his Renaissance predecessor, often repeated a refrain exactly as it had appeared before. In the couplet, however, where Le Jeune would vary the section mainly by adding voices to the texture, Messiaen used a variety of techniques, including the addition of totally new matter to the previously existing musical material. He also would transform previously used material by means of learned techniques such as diminution and augmentation. The introductions and codas were Messiaen's own innovations to the form.

Cinq rechants

But the poetic text, in contrast to the music, is more disjunctive and more opaque than in fact any of Messiaen's previous texts for his music (e.g., *Trois Mélodies, Poémes pour Mi, Chants de Terre et de Ciel, Harawi*). The French text, as we have seen, is not easy to explicate, and the addition of words in the synthetic language and even of the spoken sounds "t k t k" adds to the mystery. The rejection of normal syntactical constructions and logic shows both a desire to keep some thoughts private and a wish to show that only in a language that aspires to the nonverbal state of music can the deepest feelings be expressed. The use of words here, as in *Harawi*, is deliberately at the opposite pole from scientific language, as we might expect from a composer who had argued against scientific positivism and found it an inadequate way to truth.

The paradox inherent in Messiaen's text indicates that in his view the positive and negative psychological qualities attendant on love—the attraction, as if involuntary or set in motion by a love potion, between a man and a woman—must exist together more or less in the same space and time. As in the previous portions of the Tristan trilogy, love involves a process, a working out, an ultimate neutralizing of the negative in favor of the positive. If disintegration occurs under the shattering force of love, reintegration is bound to occur. The enclosing nature of love leads to a new freedom, though not in a straight line, not without much emotional moving back and forth between tenderness and joy, on the one hand, and fear and even terror, on the other. The texts and the music together achieve a kind of kaleidoscopic shifting of planes and surfaces, capturing the elusive meaning of the text within the "deforming prism" of Messiaen's musical language, now depending more heavily on the tritone for his melodic and harmonic material and on Indian *talas* for his rhythmic material.

The Tristan trilogy cannot fully resolve all the problems concomitant on an analysis of the myth in music. If one of the subthemes throughout has been the problem of time, Messiaen achieved his greatest success as a composer in destroying and transcending the inexorable sense of Western chronological or "clock" time in his music. The fast pace of the music in *Cinq rechants* may stand for life's briefness, as the composer himself suggested,[46] but this does not mean that he has set aside his theological and eschatological concerns. He has merely attempted to come to terms with the abyss that may be time, the grace of God, human misery, or the sense of one's own uselessness, and he accepted the inevitability of human mortality. Human love, like life itself, is given its meaning through the knowledge of its fragility.

130   Olivier Messiaen and the Tristan Myth

NOTES

1. Malcolm Hayes, "Instrumental, Orchestral and Choral Works to 1948," in *The Messiaen Companion*, ed. Peter Hill (London: Faber and Faber, 1994), 195. The date of completion of *Cinq rechants* was December 1948. The first performance was in 1949 by the Chorale Marcel Couraud (*Olivier Messiaen: A Bibliographical Catalogue of Messiaen's Works* [Tutzing: Hans Schneider, 1998], 103). For the vocal score see Olivier Messiaen, *Cinq rechants* (Paris: Rouart, Lerolle [distrib. Éditions Salabert], 1949; copyright 1960 by Rouart-Lerolle/Salabert). Quotations, translations, and musical examples in this chapter are by kind authorization of Éditions Salabert.

2. Robert Sherlaw Johnson, *Messiaen* (London: J. M. Dent, 1975), 95; see also Johnson's Table 1 (ibid., 99).

3. Olivier Messiaen, *Music and Color: Conversations with Claude Samuel*, trans. E. Thomas Glasgow (Portland, Oregon: Amadeus Press, 1994), 129.

4. Olivier Messiaen, program notes accompanying *Cinq rechants* (long-playing record, recorded under the composer's artistic direction, reissued as Musical Heritage MHS 1187); see also Messiaen, *Music and Color*, 129.

5. Wilfrid Mellers, *Caliban Reborn* (London: Gollancz, 1968), 102.

6. Pierrette Mari, *Olivier Messiaen* (Paris: Seghers, 1965), 50.

7. Antoine Goléa, *Rencontres avec Olivier Messiaen* (Paris: Julliard, 1960), 180. Perhaps Messiaen was thinking of Rilke's Ninth Elegy: "Also vor allem das Schwersein, also der Liebe lange Erfahrung,—also lauter Unsägliches" ("Above all, the hardness of life, the long experience of love; in fact, purely untellable things" (*Duino Elegies*, ed. and trans. J. B. Leishman and Stephen Spender [New York: W. W. Norton, 1939], 74–75).

8. See Nahma Sandrow, *Surrealism: Theatre, Arts, Ideas* (New York: Harper and Row, 1972), 31.

9. This image was specifically identified with Bosch's painting by Messiaen; see Goléa, *Rencontres*, 181.

10. See Goléa, *Rencontres*, 180.

11. André Breton, *Nadja*, trans. Richard Howard (New York: Grove Press, 1960), 160.

12. See, for example, Anna Balakian, *The Literary Origins of Surrealism* (New York: New York University Press, 1947), passim.

13. Pierre Reverdy, *Selected Poems*, ed. Timothy Bent, trans. John Ashberry et al. (Winston-Salem, N.C.: Wake Forest University Press, 1991), 42–43.

14. Messiaen, Program notes accompanying *Cinq rechants* (MHS 1187).

15. Goléa, *Rencontres*, 181.

16. Isidore of Seville, *Etymologiarum*, 3:22, as quoted in translation in *Source Readings in Music History*, ed. Oliver Strunk (New York: Norton, 1950), 98.

17. See Messiaen, *Music and Color*, 109, 178.

18. See Robert Graves, *The Greek Myths*, 2 vols. (Baltimore: Penguin, 1960), 1: 237–41.

19. See *Ariane et Barbe-Bleu*, in Maurice Maeterlinck, *Théâtre*, vol. 3 (Paris and Geneva: Resources, 1979); for a translation, see Maeterlinck, *Sister Beatrice and*

Cinq rechants 131

Ardiane and Barbe Bleu, trans. Bernard Miall (New York: Dodd, Mead, 1911), 93–183.

20. For Messiaen's indebtedness to Dukas, see, for example, Rollo Myers, *Modern French Music* (New York: Praeger, 1971), 156; Mari, *Olivier Messiaen,* 26.

21. Myers, *Modern French Music,* 58–59.

22. Gustave Samazeuilh, "Paul Dukas," *Grove's Dictionary of Music and Musicians,* 5th ed., ed. Eric Blom, 10 vols. (New York: St. Martin's Press, 1954–61), 2: 797.

23. Pierre Boulez, *Le soleil des eux: deux poèmes de René Char* (Paris: Heugel, n.d. [1948]), 1–15. For the date of this composition, see G.W. Hopkins, "Pierre Boulez," *The New Grove Dictionary of Music and Musicians,* ed. Stanley Sadie, 20 vols. (London: Macmillan, 1980), 3:101, 106.

24. Messiaen, Program notes accompanying *Cinq rechants* (MHS 1187).

25. Quoted by Gaston Bachelard, *The Poetics of Space,* trans. Maria Jolas (1964; reprint Boston: Beacon Press, 1969), 183. I have not yet been able to trace this quotation.

26. O. V. de L. Milosz, *L'Amoureuse Initiation* (Paris: Bernard Grasset, 1910), 155, 168, as quoted by Bachelard, *The Poetics of Space,* 190.

27. Messiaen, Program notes accompanying *Cinq rechants* (MHS 1187); see Claude le Jeune, *Le Printemps,* in *Les Maîtres musiciens de la renaissance française,* ed. Henry Expert, 15 vols. (New York: Broude, n.d.), vols. 12–14. The Greek meters utilized by Le Jeune, who participated in the sixteenth-century Académie's attempt to revive the classical forms of antiquity, also make an appearance in *Cinq rechants;* see Johnson, *Messiaen,* 97; Paul Griffiths, *Olivier Messiaen and the Music of Time* (Ithaca: Cornell University Press, 1985), 140–41; Carla Huston Bell, *Olivier Messiaen* (Boston: Twayne, 1984), 92–96.

28. Mellers, *Caliban Reborn,* 103.

29. Goléa, *Recontres,* 176.

30. See for convenience Friedrich Gennrich, ed., *Troubadours, Trouvères, Minne- und Meistersinger* (Cologne: Arno Volk, 1960), 12, 14; a translation of the song by Jaufre is available in James J. Wilhelm, *Seven Troubadours* (University Park: Pennsylvania State University Press, 1970), 90–91.

31. Text and translation in *Lyrics of the Troubadours and Trouvères,* ed. and trans. Frederick Golden (Garden City, N.Y.: Doubleday, 1973), 278–83.

32. Peter Dronke, *The Medieval Lyric* (New York: Harper and Row, 1969), 176.

33. Jonathan Saville, *The Medieval Erotic Alba* (New York: Columbia University Press, 1972), 90–98.

34. Translation in Wilhelm, *Seven Troubadours,* 91.

35. Ibid., 90.

36. Goléa, *Rencontres,* 176–77.

37. Messiaen, Program notes accompanying *Cinq rechants* (MHS 1187).

38. These were said by Messiaen (ibid.) to refer to Tristan's castle of glass. He seems to have been mistaken about his sources, though a crystal bed appears in the grotto that Tristan and Isolde share in Gottfried's account.

39. Messiaen, Program notes accompanying *Cinq rechants* (MHS 1187). For a chart laying out Messiaen's use of Indian *talas* in *Cinq rechants,* see Johnson, *Messiaen,* 99.

132   Olivier Messiaen and the Tristan Myth

40. Joanny Grosset, "Histoire de la musique: Inde," *Encyclopédie de la musique et Dictionnaire du Conservatoire*, ed. A. Lavignac (Paris: Delagrave, 1913–31), 1:1: 301–2.

41. Messiaen knew the orchestral score of *The Afternoon of a Faun* intimately and played it from score on the piano for his students at the conservatory, as Yvonne Loriod has reported ("Interview with Yvonne Loriod," 289).

42. Grosset, "Histoire de la musique: Inde," 301.

43. Ibid.

44. John Hollander, *The Untuning of the Sky* (Princeton: Princeton University Press, 1961), pl. [3] following p. 242.

45. Mellers, *Caliban Reborn*, 103.

46. Messiaen, Program notes accompanying *Cinq rechants* (MHS 1187).

Bibliography

WORKS BY OLIVIER MESSIAEN CITED IN THIS BOOK

Cinq rechants. Paris: Rouart, Lerolle [distr. Éditions Salabert], 1949.
Harawi: Chant d'amour et de mort. Paris: Alphonse Leduc [1948].
Poèmes pour Mi. Paris: Éditions Durand, 1939.
Quatuor pour la Fin du Temps. Paris: Éditions Durand, 1942.
The Technique of My Musical Language, trans. John Satterfield. 2 vols. Paris: Alphonse Leduc, 1956.
Turangalîla-symphonie, revised ed. Paris: Éditions Durand, 1992.
Vingt regards sur l'enfant Jésus. Paris: Éditions Durand, 1957.

PROGRAM NOTES BY OLIVIER MESSIAEN ACCOMPANYING RECORDINGS

Cinq rechants. Musical Heritage MHS 1187 (long-playing record).
Harawi. Koch International KIC-CD-7292 (compact disc).
Turangalîa-symphonie. Deutsche Grammophon 431 781–2 (compact disc).

BIBLIOGRAPHICAL CATALOGUE

Olivier Messiaen: A Bibliographical Catalogue of Messiaen's Works. Tutzing: Hans Schneider, 1998.

SECONDARY SOURCES

Bachelard, Gaston. *The Poetics of Space*, trans. Maria Jolas. 1964; reprint Boston: Beacon Press, 1969.

Baker, Robert H. *Astronomy*, 7th ed. Princeton: Van Nostrand, 1959.

Balakian, Anna. *The Literary Origins of Surrealism*. New York: New York University Press, 1947.

Basham, A. L. *The Wonder That Was India*. 1954; reprint New York: Grove Press, 1959.

Bédier, Joseph. *The Romance of Tristan and Iseult*, trans. Hillaire Belloc. New York: Albert and Charles Boni, 1927.

Bell, Carla Huston. *Olivier Messiaen*. Boston: Twayne, 1984.

Bergson, Henri. *Duration and Simultaneity*, trans. Leon Jacobson. 2nd ed. London: Clinamen Press, 1999.

Bernard, Jonathan W. "Messiaen's Synaesthesia: The Correspondence between Color and Sound in His Music," *Music Perception* 4 (1986): 41–68.

Béroul. *Le Roman de Tristan*, ed. Ernest Muret. Paris: Champion, 1967.

———. *The Romance of Tristan*, trans. Alan S. Fedrick. Baltimore: Penguin, 1970.

Blom, Eric, ed. *Grove's Dictionary of Music and Musicians*, 5th ed. 10 vols. New York: St. Martin's Press, 1954–61.

Boulez, Pierre. *Le soleil des eux: deux poémes de René Char*. Paris: Heugel, n.d. [1948].

Brereton, Geoffrey. *An Introduction to French Poets*. Fair Lawn, N.J.: Essential Books, 1957.

Breton, André. *Poems*, ed. and trans. Jean-Pierre Cauvin and Mary Ann Caws. Austin: University of Texas Press, 1982.

———. *Nadja*, trans. Richard Howard. New York: Grove Press, 1960.

Bruhn, Siglind, ed. *Messiaen's Language of Mystical Love*. New York: Garland, 1998.

Buñuel, Luis. *L'Age d'Or and Un Chien Andalou*, trans. Marianne Alexandre. New York: Simon and Schuster, 1968.

Burckhardt, Titus. *Alchemy*, trans. William Stoddart. Baltimore: Penguin, 1971.

Burkat, Leonard. "Current Chronicle," *Musical Quarterly* 36 (1950): 259–68.

Campbell, Joseph. *The Masks of God: Creative Mythology*. New York: Viking, 1968.

Coomaraswamy, Ananda K. *The Dance of Shiva*, revised ed. New York: Noonday, 1957.

Cooper, Martin. *French Music from the Death of Berlioz to the Death of Fauré*. London: Oxford University Press, 1951.

Daniélou, Alain. *The Raga-s of Northern Indian Music*. London: Barrie and Rockliff, 1968.

Dante Alighieri. *La Vita Nuova*, trans. Barbara Reynolds. Harmondsworth: Penguin, 1969.

Davidson, Audrey Ekdahl. "Olivier Messiaen's Tristan Trilogy: Time and Transcendence." Unpublished Ph.D. dissertation. University of Minnesota, 1975.

Drew, David. "Messiaen—A Provisional Study," *The Score and I.M.A. Magazine*, no. 10 (Dec. 1954): 33–49 (pt. I); no. 13 (Sept. 1955): 59–73 (pt. II); no. 14 (Dec. 1955): 41–61 (pt. III).

Bibliography   135

Dronke, Peter. *The Medieval Lyric*. New York: Harper and Row, 1969.
Eilhart von Oberge. *Tristant*, trans. J. W. Thomas. Lincoln: University of Nebraska Press, 1978.
Eliade, Mircea. *Shamanism: Archaic Techniques of Ecstasy*, trans. Willard R. Trask. Bollingen Series 76. Princeton: Princeton University Press, 1972.
————. *The Two and the One*, trans. J. M. Cohen. New York: Harper and Row, 1965.
Expert, Henry, ed. *Les Maîtres musiciens de la renaissance française*. 15 vols. New York: Broude, n.d.
Ferguson, George. *Signs and Symbols in Christian Art*. 1954; reprint Oxford University Press, 1961.
Gavoty, Bernard, and Olivier Messiaen. "Who Are You, Olivier Messiaen?" *Tempo* 58 (Summer 1961): 33–36.
Gennrich, Friedrich, ed. *Troubadours, Trouvères, Minne- und Meistersinger*. Cologne: Arno Volk, 1960.
Gibson, Walter S. *Hieronymus Bosch*. New York: Praeger, 1973.
Golden, Frederick, ed. and trans. *Lyrics of the Troubadours and Trouvères*. Garden City: Doubleday, 1973.
Goléa, Antoine. "Das Weltbild des Komponisten Olivier Messiaen," *Neue Zeitschrift für Musik* 130 (1969): 22–25.
————. *Rencontres avec Olivier Messiaen*. Paris: Julliard, 1960.
Gottfried von Strassburg. *Das Tristan-Epos*, ed. Wolfgang Spiewok. Berlin: Akademie-Verlag, 1989.
————. *Tristan*, trans. A. T. Hatto. Baltimore: Penguin, 1960.
Graves, Robert. *The Greek Myths*. 2 vols. Baltimore: Penguin, 1960.
Griffiths, Paul. *Olivier Messiaen and the Music of Time*. Ithaca: Cornell University Press, 1985.
Grosset, Joanny. "Histoire de la musique: Inde." *Encyclopédie de la musique et Dictionnaire du Conservatoire*, ed. A. Lavignac. Paris: Delagrave, 1913–31. 1:1:257–376.
Hanslick, Eduard. *Music Criticisms 1846–99*, trans. Henry Pleasants. Baltimore: Penguin, 1963.
Harcourt, Raoul d', and Marguerite d'Harcourt. *La Musique des Incas et ses survivances*. 2 vols. Paris: Paul Geuthner, 1925.
Hill, Peter, ed. *The Messiaen Companion*. London: Faber and Faber, 1994.
Hollander, John. *The Untuning of the Sky*. Princeton: Princeton University Press, 1961.
Janson, H. W. *Apes and Ape Lore in the Middle Ages and Renaissance*. London: Warburg Institute, 1952.
Johnson, Robert Sherlaw. *Messiaen*. London: J. M. Dent, 1975.
Jung, Carl G. *The Psychology of Transference*, trans. R.F.C. Hull. Bollingen Series 20. Princeton: Princeton University Press, 1969.
————, ed. *Man and His Symbols*. Garden City, N.Y.: Doubleday, 1964.
Kerman, Joseph. *Opera as Drama*, revised ed. Berkeley and Los Angeles: University of California Press, 1988.
Leeuw, Gerardus van der. *Religion in Essence and Manifestation*, trans. J. E. Turner. 2 vols. New York: Harper and Row, 1963.

136   Bibliography

Lévi-Strauss, Claude. *The Raw and the Cooked*, trans. John and Doreen Weightman. New York: Harper and Row, 1969.
Lockspeiser, Edward. *Debussy: His Life and Mind*, 2 vols. New York: Macmillan, 1962.
Loomis, Roger Sherman. *The Development of Arthurian Romance*. 1963; reprint New York: W. W. Norton, 1970.
Maeterlinck, Maurice. *Théâtre*. Vol. 3. Paris and Geneva: Resources, 1979.
———. *Sister Beatrice and Ardiane and Barbe Bleu*, trans. Bernard Miall. New York: Dodd, Mead, 1911.
Mallarmé, Stéphane. *Selected Poems*, ed. C. F. MacIntyre. Berkeley and Los Angeles: University of California Press, 1965.
Mari, Pierrette. *Olivier Messiaen*. Paris: Seghers, 1965.
Mellers, Wilfrid. *Caliban Reborn*. London: Gollancz, 1968.
———. *François Couperin and the French Classical Tradition*. New York: Dover, 1968.
Mérimée, Prosper. *The Venus of Ille and Other Stories*, trans. Jean Kimber. London: Oxford University Press, 1966.
Messiaen, Olivier. *Music and Color: Conversations with Claude Samuel*, trans. E. Thomas Glasgow. Portland, Oregon: Amadeus Press, 1994.
Meyer-Baer, Kathi. *The Music of the Spheres and the Dance of Death*. Princeton: Princeton University Press, 1963.
Meyers, Rollo. *Modern French Music*. New York: Praeger, 1971.
Pandey, S. M., and Norman Zide. "Sūrdās and His Krishna-*Bhakti*." In *Krishna: Myths, Rites, and Attitudes*, ed. Milton Singer. Honolulu: East-West Center Press, 1966.
Panofsky, Erwin. *Studies in Iconology*. 1939; reprint New York: Harper and Row, 1962.
Poe, Edgar Allan. *The Complete Works*, ed. James A. Harrison. 17 vols. 1902; reprint New York: AMS Press, 1965.
Quénetain, Tanneguy de. "Messiaen, Poet of Nature," *Music and Musicians* 11 (May 1963): 8–12.
Quinones, Ricardo. *The Renaissance Discovery of Time*. Cambridge: Harvard University Press, 1972.
Réau, Louis. *Iconographie de l'art Chrétien*, 3 vols. Paris: Presses Universitaires de France, 1956.
Reverdy, Pierre. *Selected Poems*, ed. Timothy Bent; trans. John Ashberry et al. Winston-Salem: Wake Forest University Press, 1991.
Rilke, Rainer Maria. *Duino Elegies*, ed. and trans. J. B. Leishman and Stephen Spender. New York: W. W. Norton, 1939.
Rössler, Almut. *Contributions to the Spiritual World of Olivier Messiaen with Original Texts by the Composer*, trans. Barbara Dagg and Nancy Poland. Duisburg: Gilles and Francke, 1986.
Rostand, Claude. *Olivier Messiaen*. Paris: Ventadour, 1957.
Rubin, William S. *Dada, Surrealism, and Their Heritage*. New York: Museum of Modern Art, 1968.
Sadie, Stanley, ed. *The New Grove Dictionary of Music and Musicians*. 20 vols. London: Macmillan, 1980.

Bibliography 137

Samuel, Claude. *Entretiens avec Olivier Messiaen*. Paris: Belfond, 1967.

Sandrow, Nahma. *Surrealism: Theatre, Arts, Ideas*. New York: Harper and Row, 1972.

Sargent, Winthrop. "Types of Quechua Melody," *Musical Quarterly* 20 (1934): 230–45.

Saville, Jonathan. *The Medieval Erotic Alba*. New York: Columbia University Press, 1972.

Schmalenbach, Werner. *Chagall*, trans. M. Ledivelec. Milan: Uffizi Press, n.d.

Sebeok, Thomas A., ed. *Myth: A Symposium*. Philadelphia: American Folklore Society, 1955.

Smalley, Roger. "Debussy and Messiaen," *Musical Times* 109 (1968): 128–31.

Spies, Werner. *Max Ernst–Loplop: The Artist's Other Self*, trans. George Braziller. London: Thames and Hudson, 1983.

———, and Helmut Rudolf Leppien. *Max Ernst Oeuvre-Katalog*. 3 vols. Cologne: DuMont Schauberg, 1975.

Stevenson, Robert. *Music in Aztec and Inca Territory*. Berkeley and Los Angeles: University of California Press, 1968.

Strayer Joseph, ed. *The Encyclopedia of the Middle Ages*. 13 vols. New York: Charles Scribner's Sons, 1984–89.

Strunk, Oliver. *Source Readings in Music History*. New York: W. W. Norton, 1950.

Tenzer, Michael. *Balinese Music*. Berkeley and Singapore: Periplus Editions, 1991.

Wagner, Richard. *Tristan und Isolde*, ed. Isolde Vetter. Sämtliche Werke 8, pts. 1–3. Mainz: B. Schott's Söhne, 1990.

———. *Tristan und Isolde*. Leipzig: Breitkopf und Härtel, n.d. [c. 1880].

———. *Tristan and Isolde*, trans. Stewart Robb. New York: Dutton, 1965.

Waldberg, Patrick. *Surrealism*. New York: McGraw-Hill, n.d.

Waumsley, Stuart. *The Organ Music of Olivier Messiaen*, 2nd ed. Paris: Leduc, 1975.

Whittall, Arnold. "Stravinsky and Music Drama," *Music and Letters* 50 (1969): 63–67.

Wilhelm, James J. *Seven Troubadours*. University Park: Pennsylvania State University Press, 1970.

Zimmermann, Heinz Werner. "Ein Gespräch mit Olivier Messiaen," *Musik und Kirche* 39 (1969): 38–39.

———. "The Technique of Messiaen's 'La Nativité du Seigneur'," trans. Audrey Davidson, *Universitas: A Journal of Religion and the University* 4 (1966): 123–33.

Zuckerkandl, Victor. *Sound and Symbol*, trans. Willard Trask. Bollingen Series, 44. 1956; reprint Princeton: Princeton University Press, 1969.

Index

Abyss, as symbol, 6, 24, 30–31, 33, 39, 51, 91, 96, 129; of despair, 23; of Hades, 111; of human misery and of divine grace, 29, 97; of time, 29–30, 33, 39, 97

Alba (dawn song), 11, 25, 27, 29, 45–46, 110, 115. *See also* Guiraut de Bornehl

Alchemy, 74–75, 86–87

Andes. *See* Mountains

Apel, Willi, 83

Ariadne, 112

Ariane et Barbe Bleu. See Dukas, Paul; Maeterlinck, Maurice

Aristotle, 93

Baader, Franz von, 94

Bach, Johann Sebastian, 15

Bachelard, Gaston, 114–15

Barker, Noelle, 59 n.2

Bartók, Béla, 13

Bédier, Joseph, 90

Beethoven, Ludwig van, 16, 100

Bergson, Henri, on time and duration, 9, 17, 125

Berlioz, Hector, composer of *Roméo et Juliette*, 79

Bernstein, Leonard, 101 n.1

Béroul, 1, 5, 90

Birds, bird song, 8, 16, 24, 26–28, 30–31, 33, 42, 48, 51–54, 57, 59, 62 n.65, 63, 83–84, 90–91, 93, 114, 127; birds as messengers, 28. *See also* Dove

Bluebeard, 112, 114, 118

Boehme, Jacob, 94

Boris Godunov. See Mussorgsky, Modeste

Bosch, Hieronymus, painter of *Garden of Earthly Delights*, xiii, 10, 24, 66, 68, 90, 109, 113–14, 119, 121

Boulez, Pierre, setting of René Char, "Complainte du lézard amoureux," 113

Brangäne, character in Tristan story, 11, 43, 45, 110, 114, 117–18

Breton, André, 7; author of poem "L'Union Libre," 68, 85–87, 100, 109
Bruckner, Anton, 100
Bunlet, Marcelle, 59 n.2
Buñuel, Luis. *See* Dali, Salvador
Burkat, Leonard, 77, 98

Calder, Alexander, 69
Celtic sources of Tristan story, 1, 20 n.43, 67
Chagall, Marc, 68, 109; painter of *The Red Sun*, 85
Chant-rechant, 80, 108–9, 111, 113–15, 117, 119–20, 122, 124–25
Char, René. *See* Boulez, Pierre
Chung, Myung-Whun, 101 n.2
Colombe verte. *See* Dove
Colors, symbolic, 18 n.11, 25; black, 29–30, 36, 38–39; blue, 37, 72; blue orange, 33; blue violet (Love of Truth), 25, 72; garnet, red, 33, 36–37, 72; gold, 37; green, 28, 47–48, 57; mauve, 36, 47–48; red-violet (Truth of Love), 25, 29–30, 72; turquoise, 33; violet, 25, 29–30, 33, 72
Coomaraswamy, Ananda, 64
Copernicus, 126
Couperin, François, 80
Couplet, 80–90, 115, 117, 118–21, 123–24, 128
Cubism, 85, 101, 109

Dali, Salvador, painter of *Persistence of Memory*, 8; collaboration with Luis Buñuel on film *Un Chien Andalou*, 37, 56
Danäe, 112
Dance, cosmic. *See* Lîla
Dante Alighieri, 4; author of *Inferno*, 4, 42; of *La Vita nuova*, 52
Death, 11, 18, 20 n.43, 23–24, 38–39, 46–50, 109–11, 113, 117–18, 120, 125
Debussy, Claude; composer, of *Afternoon of a Faun*, 120, 132 n.41;

of *Nocturnes*, 53; of *Pelléas et Mélisande*, 13–14, 20 n.60, 25, 59–60 n.6, 96; of works for piano, 14; use of whole tone scale, 14
Deçi-talas. *See* Talas
Delbos, Claire, first wife of Olivier Messiaen, 3, 5, 52
Diabolus in musica. *See* Tritone
Don Giovanni. *See* Mozart, Wolfgang Amadeus
Dove, *colombe verte*, symbol for loved one, 12, 20 nn.53, 60, 40, 43, 49, 57–58; for infidelity, 12, 27–28, 42–43; its roulades of love, 34, 57
Drew, David, 15–16, 21 n.66, 78, 84, 88, 92, 97
Dronke, Peter, 116
Dukas, Paul, composer of opera *Ariane et Barbe Bleu*, 112–13
Duration. *See* Time

Ehlert, Ludwig, 67
Eilhart, 1, 5
Éluard, Paul, 7
Enchainment, 14, 26, 53, 59, 94
Erasmus Prize, 2
Ernst, Max, as Loplop, Superior of the Birds, 8
Eurydice, 111–12

Falla, Manuel de, 13
Flowers, as symbols, 28, 72; violet, 25, 43–44, 72, 91. *See also* Messiaen, Olivier, works: *Turangalîla-symphonie*: flower theme
Fludd, Robert, 126
Folquet de Marselha, troubadour, 115–16
Franck, César, 14
Freud, Sigmund, psychoanalytic ideas of, 7
Fruit, as symbol, 24, 28, 31, 34, 41, 48, 50, 72, 90–91

Gamelan, Balinese ensemble imitated by Messiaen, 16, 63, 78, 81–82, 88, 99

Index   141

German song, *Minnelied*, 53
Gibon, Jehan de, 60 n.6
Glass, Philip, 35
Gluck, Christoph Willibald, composer
    of *Orfeo ed Euridice*, 111
Goléa, Antoine, 3, 37, 39, 44, 56, 87
Górecki, Henryk, 17, 58
Görlitz prison camp, 2
Gottfried von Strassburg, 1, 5, 42, 52,
    90, 132 n.38
Greek metrics. *See* Metrics, Greek
Griffiths, Paul, 64
Guiraut de Bornehl, composer of
    "Reis glorios," 45–46, 115–16

Hanslick, Eduard, 41, 67
Harawi. See Messiaen, Olivier, works
harawi (also known as *yarawi*), 12–13,
    116. *See also* Peruvian folklore,
    songs
d'Harcourt, Raoul and Marguerite, 12,
    31, 34, 59, 117
Hayes, Malcolm, 63
Hepworth, Barbara, 69
Hopfen, Hans, 67

Indian rhythms. *See Talas*
d'Indy, Vincent, 14
Isidore of Seville, 111

le Jeune, Claude, composer of *Le
    Printemps*, 80, 108, 115, 124, 128,
    131 n.27
Johnson, Robert Sherlaw, 48, 107
Jung, Carl, 75

Kerman, Joseph, 11
Konārak, statues at, 87
Koussevitzky, Serge, 101 n.1
Krishna, Indian god, 65
Kurwenal, character in Tristan story,
    67

Lancelot and Guinevere, characters in
    Arthurian story, 42
Leeuw, Gerardus van der, 55
Lévi-Strauss, Claude, 101

"Ligeia." *See* Poe, Edgar Allan
Light, as symbol, 34, 44
Lîla, play, cosmic dance, 11, 32, 38, 55–
    56, 64–66, 85, 89
Lizard, lizards, as symbols, 113, 119–
    20, 124–25
Loplop. *See* Ernst, Max
Loriod, Yvonne, 1, 5, 101 n.1, 101–2
    n.2, 132 n.41
Love potion (*philter*), 6, 10, 20 n. 43,
    41–43, 66–67, 110, 120

Maeterlinck, Maurice: author of
    libretto of *Pélleas et Mélisande*, 20
    n.60, 112; author of drama *Ariane
    et Barbe-Bleu*, 112–13
Mahler, Gustav, 100
Mallarmé, Stéphane, author of
    "Afternoon of a Faun," 6–8, 120
Malory, Sir Thomas, author of *Morte
    d'Arthur*, 68, 111, 126
Manning, Jane, 59 n. 2, 61 n.65
Mari, Pierette, 17, 108
Mark, King, uncle of Tristan, 67, 110,
    126
Medusa, 111–12, 124–26
Mellers, Wilfrid, 26, 80, 88, 108, 115,
    128
Melot, character in Tristan story, 67
Mendelssohn, Felix, composer of
    Songs without Words, 79
"Merculinus," alchemist, 75
Mercury, 111
Mérimée, Prosper, author of "La
    Venus d'Ille," 68–70, 77, 85, 100,
    113
Merlin, magician in Arthurian story,
    5, 68, 111
Messiaen, Alain, brother of Olivier
    Messiaen, 9
Messiaen, Olivier: faith, 1–6; life, 1–6
Messiaen, Olivier, works:
    L'Ascension, 2, 88;
    Le Banquet céleste, 2;
    Catalogue d'Oiseaux, 28;
    Chants de Terre et de Ciel, 4, 44, 52,
    68, 129;

Index

Cinq rechants, 1, 5–7, 10–11, 13–14, 17, 20 n.43, 23–24, 59, 66–68, 79–80, 90, 107–32;

Le Corps glorieux, 2, 13, 29;

Harawi: Chant d'amour et de mort, 1, 3–5, 8, 10–14, 17, 22–64, 66–69, 72, 76, 79, 84–85, 91, 107–8, 113, 115–17, 125, 127–29; Song 1: "La ville qui dormait, toi," 11, 24–27, 52, 72; Song 2: "Bonjour toi, colombe verte," 14, 24, 27–29, 34, 41–43, 45, 58, 70, 91; Song 3: "Montagnes," 23–24, 29–30, 38–39, 91; Song 4: "Doundou tchil," 23–24, 29–35, 41, 48, 58; Song 5: "L'amour de Piroutcha," 11–12, 14, 23–24, 33, 35–38, 46, 52, 57–58, 112, 125; Song 6: "Répétition planétaire," 24, 38–40, 57; Song 7: "Adieu," 10, 14, 24, 27, 40–43, 58, 67, 72; Song 8: "Syllabes," 24, 27, 34, 43–46; Song 9: "L'escalier redit, gestes du soleil," 7, 10–11, 14, 17, 23–24, 27, 38, 45–50, 58, 67, 70, 110, 112–13; Song 10: "Amour oiseau d'étoile," 8, 14, 20 n.60, 24, 41, 51–54, 91; Song 11: "Katchikatchi les étoiles," 8, 11, 24, 32, 41, 54–57, 85, 115, 125; Song 12: "Dans le noir," 14, 24, 27, 42–43, 57–59;

Livre d'Orgue, 29, 97, 128;

La Nativité du Seigneur, 2;

Poèmes pour Mi, 3–4, 13, 44, 52, 68, 129;

Quatuor pour la fin du temps, 2, 6, 29, 33, 59;

Saint François d'Assise, 2;

Technique of My Musical Language, 4, 13, 33, 57;

Trois Mélodies, 3, 129;

Turangalîla-symphonie, 1, 5–7, 10–11, 14–15, 17, 23, 31–32, 59, 63–108, 110, 113–28; chordal progression theme, 69, 74, 76, 81–82, 94–95; flower theme, 14, 69, 71–73, 76–77, 79, 83–84, 90, 94–95, 97, 101;

love theme, 14, 69, 72–74, 76, 79–84, 89, 91, 94–101; statue theme, 14, 69, 71–72, 76–78, 83–85, 87–89, 94–99;

Vingt regards sur l'enfant Jésus, 44, 46

Messiaen, Pierre, father of Olivier Messiaen, 9

Metrics, Greek, 15, 108, 131 n.27

Meyers, Rollo, 112

Milosz, O. V. de L., 115

Minnelied. *See* German song

Modes of limited transposition, 4, 13–14, 24–25, 33, 38, 59, 98

Monkey chant, 11, 27, 43, 45, 126; Balinese monkey chant (*Kečak*), 45, 61 n.45

Monteverdi, Claudio, composer of *Orfeo*, 111

Monuments, ancient Mexican, 69

Moore, Henry, 69

Morolt, character in Tristan story, 67

Mountains, as symbols, 17, 23, 29–30; Andes, 30, 37–38, 43

Mozart, Wolfgang Amadeus, 102 n.2; composer of *Don Giovanni*, 71, 101

Mussorgsky, Modeste, composer of *Boris Godunov*, 70–71, 101

Nebuchadnezzar, 57

Non-retrogradable rhythms. *See* Rhythm

Non-transposition, 33

North Indian rhythms. *See Talas*

Ollantay, Peruvian music drama, 12

Orpheus, 111–12, 117–18

Ovid, author of *Metamorphoses*, 111

Paolo and Francesca. *See* Dante Alighieri, *Inferno*

Pärt, Arno, 17, 35, 58

Pelléas et Mélisande. *See* Debussy, Claude

Penrose, Roland, painter of *The Invisible Isle* (sometimes called

Index

Seeing Is Believing), xi, 8, 51–52, 56, 61–62 n.52, 113
Pentatonicism. *See* Tonality
Perseus, 111–12, 124–26
Persistence of Memory. See Dali, Salvador
Peruvian folklore, 10, 12–13, 20 n.60, 24, 27–28, 31–32, 38, 43, 54, 59
Peruvian (Quechua) songs, 11–12, 24, 31, 59, 117; "Delirio," 27, 42, 58, 60 n.12; "Katchikatchi," 11; "Mariposača Niñača," 55; "Piruča," 12, 36–37; "Quisera," 31–33; "Tikata Tarpuinikiču," 34–35, 58; "Tungu, Tungu," 36, 57
Philtre. See Love potion
Piruça (Piroutcha), character in Peruvian folklore, 10, 12, 31, 33, 36, 43–44
"Pit and the Pendulum, The." *See* Poe, Edgar Allan
Poe, Edgar Allan, author: of "Ligeia," 68, 100, 113–14; of "The Pit and the Pendulum," 68, 76, 92, 114
Polydeuctes, 112
Polymodality, 78
Preisner, Zbigniew, 17

Quechua songs. *See* Peruvian songs
Quénetain, Tanneguy de, 5, 44

Rādhā, favored cowgirl of Krishna, 65
Rainbow, as symbol, 2–3, 23–24, 30–31, 33, 35, 45, 54
Rāmāyana, 61 n.45
Rameau, Jean-Philippe, 13
Ravel, Maurice, composer of *Bolero,* 35, 45
Revelation, book of the Bible, 2
Reverdy, Pierre, 7, 109–10
Rhythm, 15, 17, 39; added rhythms, 4, 15, 26, 55; non-retrogradable rhythms, 4, 13, 15, 33, 54–55, 66, 117; plainchant rhythms, 15. *See also Talas*

Rilke, Rainer Maria, 114; author of *Duino Elegies,* 109, 130 n.7
Rimbaud, Arthur, 6
Rodin, Auguste, 2
Roman de la Rose, 21 n.60, 60 n.14
Romeo and Juliet. See Shakespeare, William
Roméo et Juliette. See Berlioz, Hector
Rondeau, 80, 115
Rostand, Claude, 12
Rudel, Jauffre, troubadour, 115–16

Samazeuilh, Gustave, 112
Samuel, Claude, 2, 5
Sandrow, Nahma, 8
Śarngadeva, Indian music theorist, 15, 64, 66
Sauvage, Cécile, mother of Olivier Messiaen, 9; author of *L'Ame en bourgeon,* 9, "Le sourire," 3
Saville, Jonathan, 45–46, 116
Schlegel, Friedrich, 94, 104 n.72
Schmalenbach, Werner, 85
Shakespeare, William, author of *Romeo and Juliet,* 68, 85–86, 100, 115
Shelton, Lucy, 59 n.2
Shiva, dance of, 64
Smalley, Roger, 13
Song of Songs, 10
Space, 76, 78, 86, 114–15, 111, 117–18, 122, 125–26
Stars, as symbols, 8, 11, 24, 29, 31, 33–34, 38, 41–42, 51–56, 86, 91, 109, 117–20
Statue. *See* Messiaen, Olivier, works: *Turangalîla-symphonie*: statue themes
Stravinsky, Igor, 15, 20 n.59, 77
Surrealism, 3, 6–8, 12, 68, 79–80, 101, 107, 109; paintings and films, 6, 24, 36–37, 51, 56, 61 n.30. *See also* Dali, Salvador

Talas, 15, 64, 66, 76, 78, 93, 108, 118, 120, 122, 124, 128–29, 131 n.39
Tavener, John, 17, 35, 58

Tempo, 49
Tennyson, Alfred, Lord, author of
    Idylls of the King, 110–11
Theseus, 112
Thomas Aquinas, St., 21, n.81
Thomas of Brittany, 1, 5
Time, 2, 7, 15–18, 21–22 n.81, 23–24,
    29, 38–39, 45–50, 56, 58, 64–65,
    76, 78, 81, 84, 86, 97, 125–26, 128–
    29; as destroyer, 16; as duration,
    49, 58, 65; and eternity, 16–18, 84;
    timelessness, 15, 17, 65, 91, 113–
    14; urgency of, 16. *See also* Abyss
Tonality, pentatonicism, 12, 36
Tristan und Isolde. See Wagner,
    Richard
Tritone, *Diabolus in musica*, 26–27, 37,
    42, 49, 67, 77–78, 113, 116–20,
    124, 126–29
Tuning, of the spheres, 126

Venus d'Ille. *See* Mérimée, Prosper
Vivian, Viviane (Niniane, Nimue),
    character in Arthurian story, 5,
    68, 110–11, 113, 115, 121, 124–26

Wagner, Richard, composer of *Tristan
    und Isolde*, 1, 6, 9–11, 13, 24–27,
    33–34, 41, 43, 45–46, 52, 66–68,
    79, 86, 90, 101, 110
Whittall, Arnold, 13, 20 n.59

Yarawi. See Harawi

Zimmermann, Heinz Werner, 9

About the Author

AUDREY EKDAHL DAVIDSON is a Professor of Music Emerita at Western Michigan University and has published extensively on both early and modern music. She is also a musician and composer.